Teach Yourself
Microsoft®
Excel 2000

IDG's **3-D Visual**™ Series

 *From* **maranGraphics**™

IDG Books Worldwide, Inc.
An International Data Group Company
Foster City, CA • Indianapolis • Chicago • New York

Teach Yourself Microsoft® Excel 2000 VISUALLY™

Published by
IDG Books Worldwide, Inc.
An International Data Group Company
919 E. Hillsdale Blvd., Suite 400
Foster City, CA 94404

Library of Congress Catalog Card No.: 99-63953

ISBN: 0-7645-6056-5

Printed in the United States of America

10 9 8 7 6 5 4 3

Distributed in the United States by IDG Books Worldwide, Inc.

Distributed by CDG Books Canada Inc. for Canada; by Transworld Publishers Limited in the United Kingdom; by IDG Norge Books for Norway; by IDG Sweden Books for Sweden; by Woodslane Pty. Ltd. for Australia; by Woodslane (NZ) Ltd. for New Zealand; by TransQuest Publishers Pte Ltd. for Singapore, Malaysia, Thailand, Indonesia, and Hong Kong; by ICG Muse, Inc. for Japan; by Norma Comunicaciones S.A. for Colombia; by Intersoft for South Africa; by Le Monde en Tique for France; by International Thomson Publishing for Germany, Austria and Switzerland; by Distribuidora Cuspide for Argentina; by Livraria Cultura for Brazil; by Ediciones ZETA S.C.R. Ltda. for Peru; by WS Computer Publishing Corporation, Inc., for the Philippines; by Contemporanea de Ediciones for Venezuela; by Express Computer Distributors for the Caribbean and West Indies; by Micronesia Media Distributor, Inc. for Micronesia; by Grupo Editorial Norma S.A. for Guatemala; by Chips Computadoras S.A. de C.V. for Mexico; by Editorial Norma de Panama S.A. for Panama; by American Bookshops for Finland. Authorized Sales Agent: Anthony Rudkin Associates for the Middle East and North Africa.
For corporate orders, please call maranGraphics at 800-469-6616.
For general information on IDG Books Worldwide's books in the U.S., please call our Consumer Customer Service department at 800-762-2974.
For reseller information, including discounts and premium sales, please call our Reseller Customer Service department at 800-434-3422.
For information on where to purchase IDG Books Worldwide's books outside the U.S., please contact our International Sales department at 317-596-5530 or fax 317-596-5692.
For consumer information on foreign language translations, please contact our Customer Service department at 1-800-434-3422, fax 317-596-5692, or e-mail rights@idgbooks.com.
For information on licensing foreign or domestic rights, please phone 1-650-655-3109.
For sales inquiries and special prices for bulk quantities, please contact our Sales department at 650-655-3200.
For information on using IDG Books Worldwide's books in the classroom or for ordering examination copies, please contact our Educational Sales department at 800-434-2086 or fax 317-596-5499.
For press review copies, author interviews, or other publicity information, please contact our Public Relations department at 650-655-3000 or fax 650-655-3299.
For authorization to photocopy items for corporate, personal, or educational use, please contact maranGraphics at 800-469-6616.
Screen shots displayed in this book are based on pre-release software and are subject to change.

Trademark Acknowledgments

Permissions

The 3-D illustrations are the copyright of maranGraphics, Inc.

U.S. Corporate Sales	U.S. Trade Sales
Contact maranGraphics at (800) 469-6616 or Fax (905) 890-9434.	Contact IDG Books at (800) 434-3422 or (650) 655-3000.

ABOUT IDG BOOKS WORLDWIDE

Welcome to the world of IDG Books Worldwide.

IDG Books Worldwide, Inc., is a subsidiary of International Data Group, the world's largest publisher of computer-related information and the leading global provider of information services on information technology. IDG was founded more than 30 years ago by Patrick J. McGovern and now employs more than 9,000 people worldwide. IDG publishes more than 290 computer publications in over 75 countries. More than 90 million people read one or more IDG publications each month.

Launched in 1990, IDG Books Worldwide is today the #1 publisher of best-selling computer books in the United States. We are proud to have received eight awards from the Computer Press Association in recognition of editorial excellence and three from Computer Currents' First Annual Readers' Choice Awards. Our best-selling ...For Dummies® series has more than 50 million copies in print with translations in 31 languages. IDG Books Worldwide, through a joint venture with IDG's Hi-Tech Beijing, became the first U.S. publisher to publish a computer book in the People's Republic of China. In record time, IDG Books Worldwide has become the first choice for millions of readers around the world who want to learn how to better manage their businesses.

Our mission is simple: Every one of our books is designed to bring extra value and skill-building instructions to the reader. Our books are written by experts who understand and care about our readers. The knowledge base of our editorial staff comes from years of experience in publishing, education, and journalism — experience we use to produce books to carry us into the new millennium. In short, we care about books, so we attract the best people. We devote special attention to details such as audience, interior design, use of icons, and illustrations. And because we use an efficient process of authoring, editing, and desktop publishing our books electronically, we can spend more time ensuring superior content and less time on the technicalities of making books.

You can count on our commitment to deliver high-quality books at competitive prices on topics you want to read about. At IDG Books Worldwide, we continue in the IDG tradition of delivering quality for more than 30 years. You'll find no better book on a subject than one from IDG Books Worldwide.

John Kilcullen
Chairman and CEO
IDG Books Worldwide, Inc.

Steven Berkowitz
President and Publisher
IDG Books Worldwide, Inc.

Eighth Annual
Computer Press
Awards ≷1992

Ninth Annual
Computer Press
Awards ≷1993

Tenth Annual
Computer Press
Awards ≷1994

Eleventh Annual
Computer Press
Awards ≷1995

IDG is the world's leading IT media, research and exposition company. Founded in 1964, IDG had 1997 revenues of $2.05 billion and has more than 9,000 employees worldwide. IDG offers the widest range of media options that reach IT buyers in 75 countries representing 95% of worldwide IT spending. IDG's diverse product and services portfolio spans six key areas including print publishing, online publishing, expositions and conferences, market research, education and training, and global marketing services. More than 90 million people read one or more of IDG's 290 magazines and newspapers, including IDG's leading global brands — Computerworld, PC World, Network World, Macworld and the Channel World family of publications. IDG Books Worldwide is one of the fastest-growing computer book publishers in the world, with more than 700 titles in 36 languages. The "...For Dummies®" series alone has more than 50 million copies in print. IDG offers online users the largest network of technology-specific Web sites around the world through IDG.net (http://www.idg.net), which comprises more than 225 targeted Web sites in 55 countries worldwide. International Data Corporation (IDC) is the world's largest provider of information technology data, analysis and consulting, with research centers in over 41 countries and more than 400 research analysts worldwide. IDG World Expo is a leading producer of more than 168 globally branded conferences and expositions in 35 countries including E3 (Electronic Entertainment Expo), Macworld Expo, ComNet, Windows World Expo, ICE (Internet Commerce Expo), Agenda, DEMO, and Spotlight. IDG's training subsidiary, ExecuTrain, is the world's largest computer training company, with more than 230 locations worldwide and 785 training courses. IDG Marketing Services helps industry-leading IT companies build international brand recognition by developing global integrated marketing programs via IDG's print, online and exposition products worldwide. Further information about the company can be found at www.idg.com.   1/24/99

maranGraphics is a family-run business
located near Toronto, Canada.

At **maranGraphics**, we believe in producing great computer books–one book at a time.

Each maranGraphics book uses the award-winning communication process that we have been developing over the last 25 years. Using this process, we organize screen shots, text and illustrations in a way that makes it easy for you to learn new concepts and tasks.

We spend hours deciding the best way to perform each task, so you don't have to! Our clear, easy-to-follow screen shots and instructions walk you through each task from beginning to end.

Our detailed illustrations go hand-in-hand with the text to help reinforce the information. Each illustration is a labor of love–some take up to a week to draw!

We want to thank you for purchasing what we feel are the best computer books money can buy. We hope you enjoy using this book as much as we enjoyed creating it!

Sincerely,

The Maran Family

Please visit us on the web at:
www.maran.com

CREDITS

Authors:
Ruth Maran & Kelleigh Wing

Copy Editors:
Roxanne Van Damme
Jill Maran

Project Manager:
Judy Maran

**Editing &
Screen Captures:**
Raquel Scott
Janice Boyer
Michelle Kirchner
James Menzies
Frances Lea
Stacey Morrison
Emmet Mellow

Layout Designer:
Treena Lees

Illustrators:
Russ Marini
Jamie Bell
Peter Grecco
Sean Johannesen
Steven Schaerer

Screen Artists:
Jimmy Tam
Roben Ponce

Indexer:
Raquel Scott

Post Production:
Robert Maran

Editorial Support:
Michael Roney

ACKNOWLEDGMENTS

Thanks to the dedicated staff of maranGraphics, including
Jamie Bell, Cathy Benn, Janice Boyer, Francisco Ferreira,
Peter Grecco, Jenn Hillman, Sean Johannesen, Michelle Kirchner,
Wanda Lawrie, Frances Lea, Treena Lees, Jill Maran, Judy Maran,
Robert Maran, Sherry Maran, Russ Marini, Emmet Mellow,
James Menzies, Stacey Morrison, Roben Ponce, Steven Schaerer,
Raquel Scott, Jimmy Tam, Roxanne Van Damme,
Paul Whitehead and Kelleigh Wing.

Finally, to Richard Maran who originated the easy-to-use
graphic format of this guide. Thank you for your
inspiration and guidance.

TABLE OF CONTENTS

Chapter 1

Getting Started

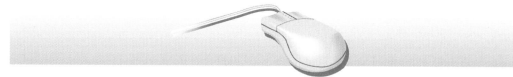

Chapter 2

Save and Open Your Workbooks

Chapter 3

Edit Your Worksheets

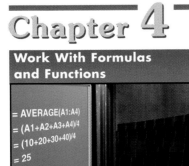

Chapter 4

Work With Formulas and Functions

= AVERAGE(A1:A4)
= (A1+A2+A3+A4)/4
= (10+20+30+40)/4
= 25

TABLE OF CONTENTS

Chapter 5

Change Your Screen Display

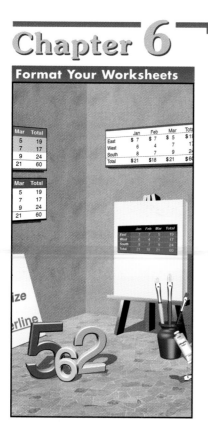

Chapter 6

Format Your Worksheets

Chapter 7

Print Your Worksheets

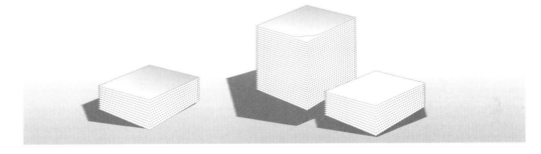

Chapter 8

Work With Multiple Worksheets

TABLE OF CONTENTS

Chapter 9

Work With Charts

Chapter 10

Work With Graphics

Chapter 11

Manage Data in a List

Chapter 12

Time-Saving Features

Chapter 13

Excel and the Internet

Microsoft Excel - Book1
File Edit View Insert Format Tools Data Window Help
Arial
12
A7
Jan 8700 1500 2336
Feb 1980 4850 4352
Mar 3850 1750 2250
Apr 1750 1980 1820
May 1920 1359 1015
Sheet1
Sheet2
Ready
NUM
HELP
Jun
Feb
Apr
Data

CHAPTER 1

Getting Started

Are you ready to begin using Microsoft Excel 2000? This chapter will help you get started.

INCOME STATEMENT			
	January	February	March
REVENUE	140,000	135,000	120,000
Payroll	35,000	35,000	35,000
Rent	5,000	5,000	5,000
Supplies	2,000	2,000	2,000
Hydro	1,000	1,000	1,000

INTRODUCTION TO EXCEL

Excel is a spreadsheet program you can use to organize, analyze and attractively present data such as a budget or sales report.

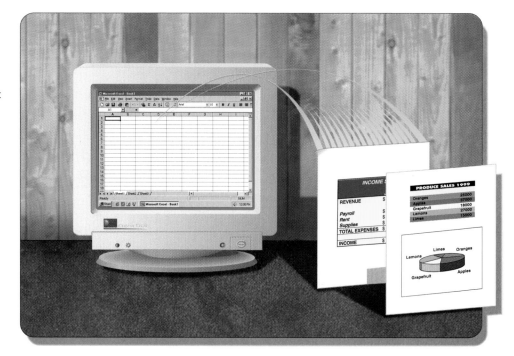

Enter and Edit Data

Excel lets you efficiently enter and edit data in a worksheet. Excel can help you quickly enter data by completing a series of numbers for you. You can add, delete or move data to a new location. You can also check a worksheet for spelling errors and instantly undo changes you regret.

Use Formulas and Functions

Formulas and functions allow you to perform calculations and analyze data in a worksheet. Common calculations include finding the sum, average or total number of items in a list.

You can also create scenarios to see how different values will affect the calculations in a worksheet.

Format Worksheets

Excel includes many formatting features that can help you change the appearance of a worksheet. You can add borders, change the color of cells, use various fonts and change the alignment of data.

ABCInc.

INCOME STATEMENT

	Jan	Feb	Mar	Total
REVENUE	$120,500	$135,500	$140,670	$395,000
Payroll	$35,000	$35,000	$35,000	$105,000
Rent	$1,200	$1,200	$1,200	$3,600
Supplies	$19,000	$21,000	$22,500	$62,500
TOTAL EXPENSES	$55,200	$77,800	$58,700	$171,100
INCOME	$65,300	$57,200	$81,970	$223,900

Print Worksheets

You can produce a paper copy of a worksheet you create. Before printing, you can see on your screen how the worksheet will look when printed. You can adjust the margins or change the orientation of the printed data.

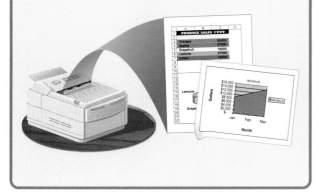

Create Charts and Graphics

Excel helps you create colorful charts from worksheet data to visually display the data. You can also create graphics, such as AutoShapes, text effects and pictures, to enhance the appearance of a worksheet and illustrate important concepts.

Manage Data in a List

Excel provides tools that help you manage and analyze a large collection of data, such as a mailing list or product list. You can sort or filter the data in a list. You can also add subtotals to summarize the data.

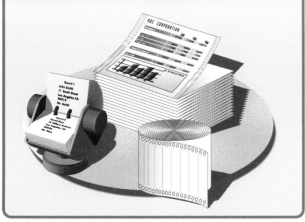

Excel and the Internet

You can save a workbook you create as a Web page. This lets you place the workbook on the Internet for other people to view. You can also add a hyperlink to a workbook to connect the workbook to a Web page.

A mouse is a handheld device that lets you select and move items on your screen.

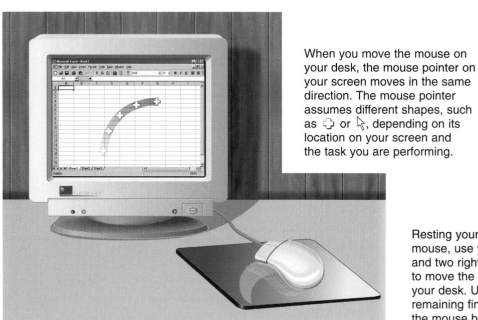

When you move the mouse on your desk, the mouse pointer on your screen moves in the same direction. The mouse pointer assumes different shapes, such as ⊕ or ↖, depending on its location on your screen and the task you are performing.

Resting your hand on the mouse, use your thumb and two rightmost fingers to move the mouse on your desk. Use your two remaining fingers to press the mouse buttons.

MOUSE ACTIONS

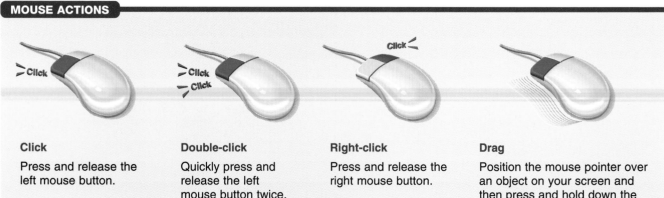

Click

Press and release the left mouse button.

Double-click

Quickly press and release the left mouse button twice.

Right-click

Press and release the right mouse button.

Drag

Position the mouse pointer over an object on your screen and then press and hold down the left mouse button. Still holding down the button, move the mouse to where you want to place the object and then release the button.

START EXCEL

When you start Excel,
a blank worksheet
appears on your
screen. You can
enter data into
this worksheet.

START EXCEL

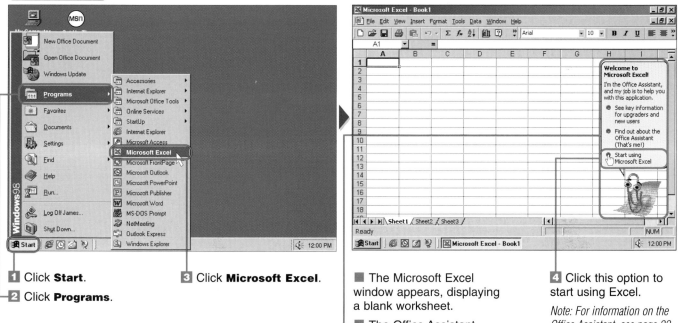

1 Click **Start**.

2 Click **Programs**.

3 Click **Microsoft Excel**.

■ The Microsoft Excel
window appears, displaying
a blank worksheet.

■ The Office Assistant
welcome appears the first
time you start Excel.

4 Click this option to
start using Excel.

*Note: For information on the
Office Assistant, see page 22.*

THE EXCEL SCREEN

The Excel screen displays several items to help you perform tasks efficiently.

Menu Bar

Provides access to lists of commands available in Excel.

Formatting Toolbar

Contains buttons to help you select common formatting commands, such as Bold and Underline.

Standard Toolbar

Contains buttons to help you select common commands, such as Save and Print.

Formula Bar

Displays the cell reference and contents of the active cell. A cell reference identifies the location of a cell in a worksheet and consists of a column letter followed by a row number, such as **A1**.

Worksheet Tabs

An Excel file is called a workbook. Each workbook is divided into several worksheets. Excel displays a tab for each worksheet.

A workbook is similar to a three-ring binder that contains several sheets of paper.

Status Bar

Displays information about the task you are performing.

WORKSHEET BASICS

An Excel worksheet consists of rows, columns and cells.

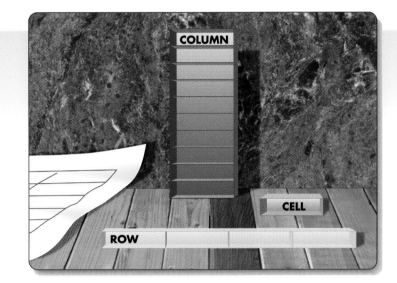

Row

A row is a horizontal line of cells. A number identifies each row (example: **3**).

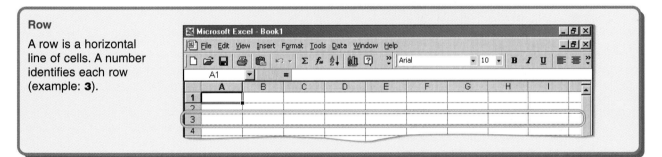

Column

A column is a vertical line of cells. A letter identifies each column (example: **B**).

Cell

A cell is the area where a row and column intersect.

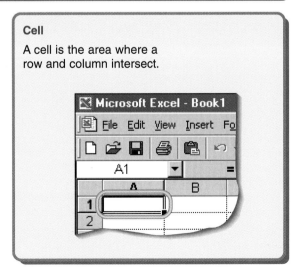

CHANGE THE ACTIVE CELL

You can make
any cell in your
worksheet the
active cell. You
enter data into
the active cell.

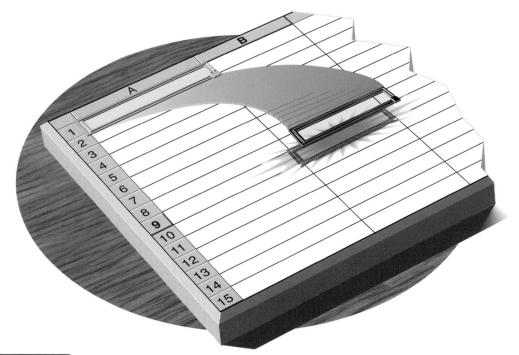

CHANGE THE ACTIVE CELL

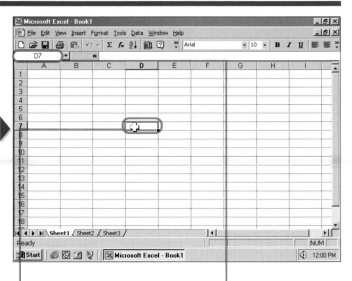

■ The active cell
displays a thick border.

■ The cell reference for
the active cell appears in
this area. A cell reference
identifies the location of
each cell in a worksheet
and consists of a column
letter followed by a row
number (example: **A1**).

1 Click the cell you want
to make the active cell.

Note: You can also press the
←, →, ↑ or ↓ key
to change the active cell.

■ The cell reference
for the new active cell
appears in this area.

A toolbar contains buttons that you can use to select commands.

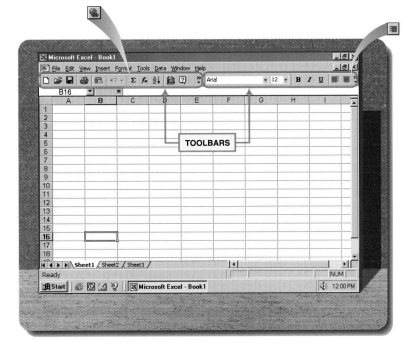

TOOLBARS

When you first start Excel, the most commonly used buttons appear on each toolbar. As you work with Excel, the toolbars automatically change to remove buttons you rarely use and display the buttons you use most often.

SELECT COMMANDS USING TOOLBARS

1 To display the name of a toolbar button, position the mouse ⌖ over the button.

■ After a few seconds, the name of the button appears in a yellow box. The button name can help you determine the task the button performs.

2 A toolbar may not be able to display all of its buttons. Click 》 to display additional buttons for the toolbar.

■ Additional buttons for the toolbar appear.

3 To use a toolbar button to select a command, click the button.

SELECT COMMANDS USING MENUS

You can select a command from a menu to perform a task. Each command performs a different task.

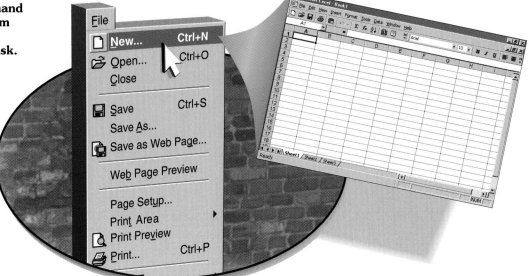

SELECT COMMANDS USING MENUS

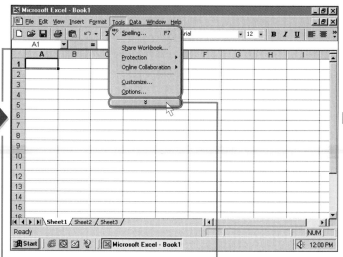

1 Click the name of the menu you want to display.

■ A short version of the menu appears, displaying the most commonly used commands.

2 To expand the menu and display all the commands, position the mouse ⤵ over ⟱.

Note: If you do not perform step 2, the expanded menu will automatically appear after a few seconds.

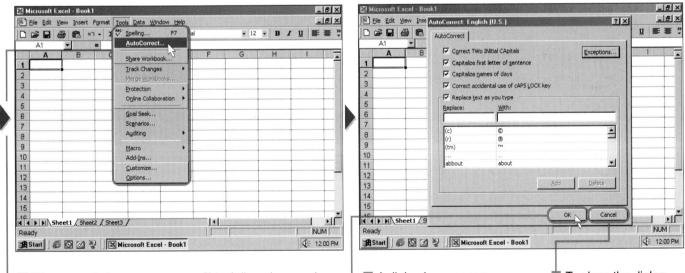

? **How can I make a command appear on the short version of a menu?**

When you select a command from an expanded menu, the command is automatically added to the short version of the menu. The next time you display the short version of the menu, the command you selected will appear.

Short menu

Expanded menu

■ The expanded menu appears, displaying all the commands.

3 Click the command you want to use.

Note: A dimmed command is currently not available.

■ To close a menu without selecting a command, click outside the menu.

■ A dialog box appears if the command you selected displays three dots (...).

4 When you finish selecting options in the dialog box, click **OK** to confirm your changes.

■ To close the dialog box without selecting any options, click **Cancel**.

ENTER DATA

You can enter data into your worksheet quickly and easily.

SALES REPORT IN UNITS

	1996	1997	1998	1999
January	10500	8850	9000	10400
February	9400	9750	9500	9850
March	6450	8450	8950	9900
April	7890	9000	9400	10850
May	8920	7359	8700	11500

ENTER DATA

1 Click the cell where you want to enter data. Then type the data.

Note: In this example, the size of data was changed from 10 point to 12 point to make the data easier to read.

■ If you make a typing mistake, press the `Backspace` key to remove the incorrect data. Then type the correct data.

■ The data you type appears in the active cell and the formula bar.

2 Press the `Enter` key to enter the data and move down one cell.

Note: To enter the data and move one cell in any direction, press the ←, →, ↑ or ↓ key.

3 Repeat steps **1** and **2** until you finish entering all your data.

14

?

Why did Excel change a number I entered?

If you type a number such as a zip code or product number, Excel may automatically change the appearance of the number. To have Excel display the number exactly as you enter it, type an apostrophe (') in front of the number. The apostrophe will not appear in your worksheet.

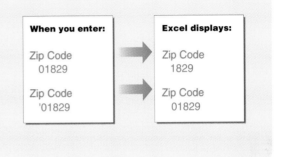

When you enter:		Excel displays:
Zip Code 01829	→	Zip Code 1829
Zip Code '01829	→	Zip Code 01829

Microsoft Excel - Sales by Location

File Edit View Insert Format Tools Data Window Help

A11   = New York

	A	B	C	D	E
1	Sales by Location				
2					
3		1996	1997	1998	Total
4	New York	$ 784,067.00	$ 196,226.00	$ 923,081.00	$ 1,903,374.00
5	Miami	$ 682,998.00	$ 173,902.00	$ 936,277.00	$ 1,793,177.00
6	Houston	$ 862,899.00	$ 804,959.00	$ 711,459.00	$ 2,379,317.00
7	Los Angeles	$ 789,397.00	$ 640,113.00	$ 837,565.00	$ 2,267,075.00
8	Phoenix	$ 991,589.00	$ 710,470.00	$ 719,170.00	$ 2,421,229.00
9	Seattle	$ 790,908.00	$ 813,509.00	$ 805,890.00	$ 2,410,307.00
10	Washington	$ 890,926.00	$ 927,899.00	$ 928,390.00	$ 2,747,215.00
11	New York				
12				Total Sales	$15,921,694.00
13					
14					
15					

Sheet1 / Sheet2 / Sheet3

Enter   NUM

Start   Microsoft Excel - Sal...   12:00 PM

AUTOCOMPLETE

■ If the first few letters you type match another cell in the column, Excel may complete the text for you.

1 To enter the text Excel provides, press the **Enter** key.

■ To enter different text, continue typing.

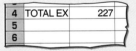

4	TOTAL EXPENSES
5	
6	

4	TOTAL EX	227
5		
6		

Long Words

If text is too long to fit in a cell, the text will spill into the neighboring cell.

If the neighboring cell contains data, Excel will display as much of the text as the column width will allow. To change the column width to display all the text, see page 68.

4	1.22E+10
5	
6	

4	#####
5	
6	

Long Numbers

If a number is too long to fit in a cell, Excel will display the number in scientific form or as number signs (#). To change the column width to display the number, see page 68.

SELECT CELLS

Before performing many tasks in Excel, you must select the cells you want to work with. Selected cells appear highlighted on your screen.

INCOME STATEMENT			
REVENUE	120,000	135,000	140,000
Payroll	32,000	32,000	32,000
Rent	5,000	5,000	5,000
Supplies	2,500	1,750	3,500
INCOME			

SELECT CELLS

SELECT A CELL

1 Click the cell you want to select.

■ The cell becomes the active cell and displays a thick border.

SELECT A GROUP OF CELLS

1 Position the mouse ✛ over the first cell you want to select.

2 Drag the mouse ✛ until you highlight all the cells you want to select.

■ To select multiple groups of cells, press and hold down the **Ctrl** key as you repeat steps **1** and **2** for each group.

■ To deselect cells, click any cell.

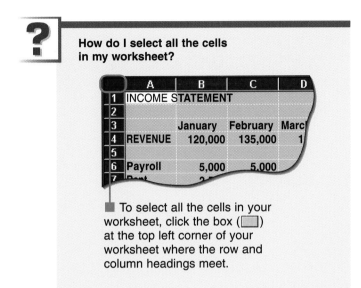

How do I select all the cells in my worksheet?

■ To select all the cells in your worksheet, click the box (☐) at the top left corner of your worksheet where the row and column headings meet.

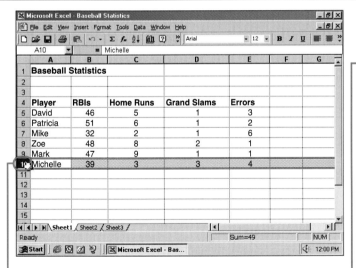

SELECT A ROW

1 Click the number of the row you want to select.

■ To select multiple rows, position the mouse ⊕ over the number of the first row you want to select. Then drag the mouse ⊕ until you highlight all the rows you want to select.

SELECT A COLUMN

1 Click the letter of the column you want to select.

■ To select multiple columns, position the mouse ⊕ over the letter of the first column you want to select. Then drag the mouse ⊕ until you highlight all the columns you want to select.

COMPLETE A SERIES

Excel can save you time by completing a text or number series for you.

You can complete a series across a row or down a column in a worksheet.

COMPLETE A TEXT SERIES

1 Enter the text you want to start the series.

2 Click the cell containing the text you entered.

3 Position the mouse over the bottom right corner of the cell (changes to +).

4 Drag the mouse + over the cells you want to include in the series.

■ The cells display the text series.

Note: If Excel cannot determine the text series you want to complete, it will copy the text in the first cell to the cells you select.

■ To deselect cells, click any cell.

18

What is the difference between a text series and a number series?

Mon	Tue	Wed	Thu
Product 1	Product 2	Product 3	Product 4
1st Quarter	2nd Quarter	3rd Quarter	4th Quarter

1996	1997	1998	1999
5	10	15	20
202	204	206	208

■ Excel completes a text series based on the text in the first cell.

■ Excel completes a number series based on the numbers in the first two cells. These numbers tell Excel how much to add to each number to complete the series.

COMPLETE A NUMBER SERIES

1 Enter the first two numbers you want to start the series.

2 Select the cells containing the numbers you entered. To select cells, see page 16.

3 Position the mouse over the bottom right corner of the selected cells (changes to +).

4 Drag the mouse + over the cells you want to include in the series.

■ The cells display the number series.

■ To deselect cells, click any cell.

SCROLL THROUGH A WORKSHEET

If your worksheet contains a lot of data, your computer screen may not be able to display all the data at once. You must scroll through your worksheet to view other areas of the worksheet.

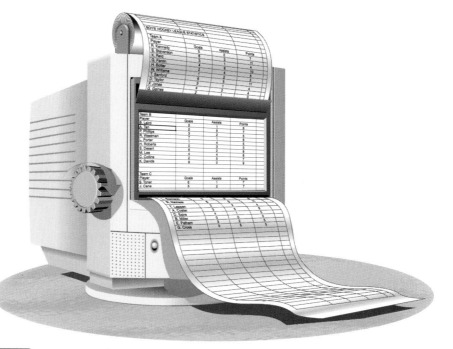

SCROLL THROUGH A WORKSHEET

SCROLL UP OR DOWN

■ To scroll up one row, click ▲.

■ To scroll down one row, click ▼.

1 To quickly scroll to any row in the worksheet, position the mouse ⩗ over the scroll box.

2 Drag the scroll box along the scroll bar until a yellow box displays the number of the row you want to appear at the top of the worksheet.

20

?

How do I use a wheeled mouse to scroll through my worksheet?

A wheeled mouse has a wheel between the left and right mouse buttons. Moving this wheel lets you quickly scroll through your worksheet. The Microsoft IntelliMouse is a popular example of a wheeled mouse.

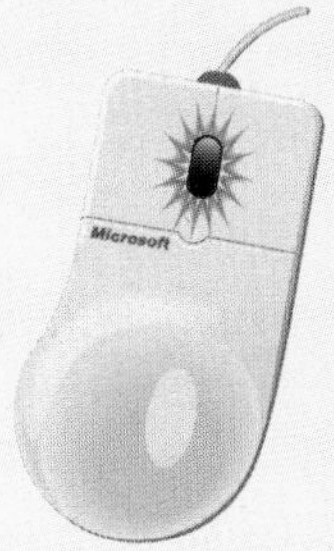

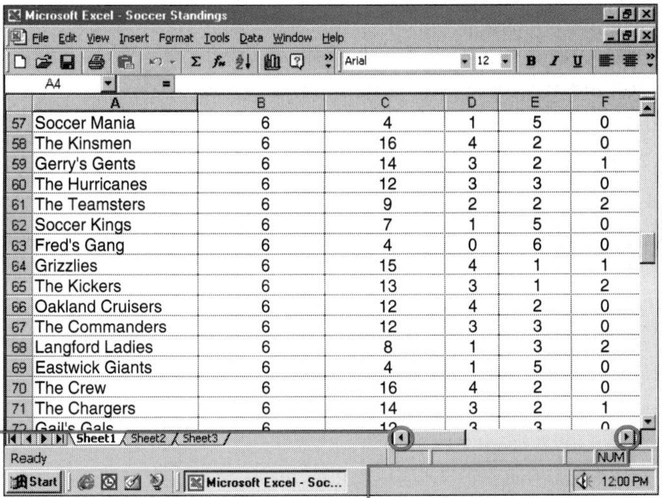

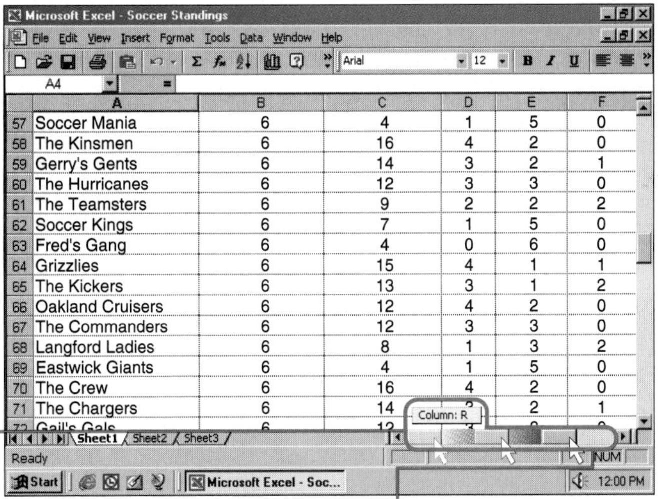

	A	B	C	D	E	F
57	Soccer Mania	6	4	1	5	0
58	The Kinsmen	6	16	4	2	0
59	Gerry's Gents	6	14	3	2	1
60	The Hurricanes	6	12	3	3	0
61	The Teamsters	6	9	2	2	2
62	Soccer Kings	6	7	1	5	0
63	Fred's Gang	6	4	0	6	0
64	Grizzlies	6	15	4	1	1
65	The Kickers	6	13	3	1	2
66	Oakland Cruisers	6	12	4	2	0
67	The Commanders	6	12	3	3	0
68	Langford Ladies	6	8	1	3	2
69	Eastwick Giants	6	4	1	5	0
70	The Crew	6	16	4	2	0
71	The Chargers	6	14	3	2	1
72	Gail's Gals	6	12	3	3	0

SCROLL LEFT OR RIGHT

■ To scroll left one column, click ◄.

■ To scroll right one column, click ►.

1 To quickly scroll to any column in the worksheet, position the mouse ⩒ over the scroll box.

2 Drag the scroll box along the scroll bar until a yellow box displays the letter of the column you want to appear at the left side of the worksheet.

GETTING HELP

If you do not know
how to perform a
task, you can ask
the Office Assistant
for help.

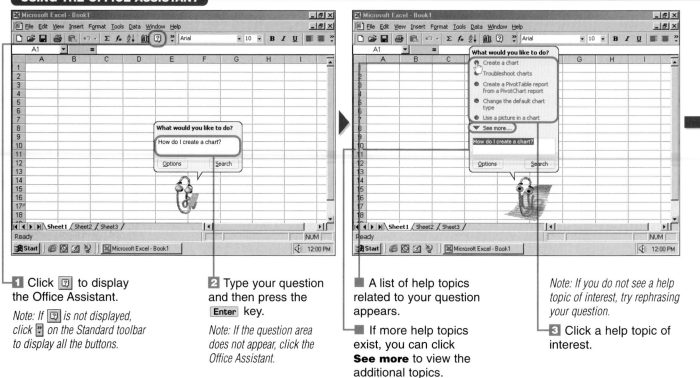

1 Click 🔲 to display
the Office Assistant.

*Note: If 🔲 is not displayed,
click 🔹 on the Standard toolbar
to display all the buttons.*

2 Type your question
and then press the
`Enter` key.

*Note: If the question area
does not appear, click the
Office Assistant.*

■ A list of help topics
related to your question
appears.

■ If more help topics
exist, you can click
See more to view the
additional topics.

*Note: If you do not see a help
topic of interest, try rephrasing
your question.*

3 Click a help topic of
interest.

Can I move the Office Assistant?

If the Office Assistant covers information on your screen, you may need to move the Office Assistant. Position the mouse ⌖ over the Office Assistant and then drag the Office Assistant to a new location.

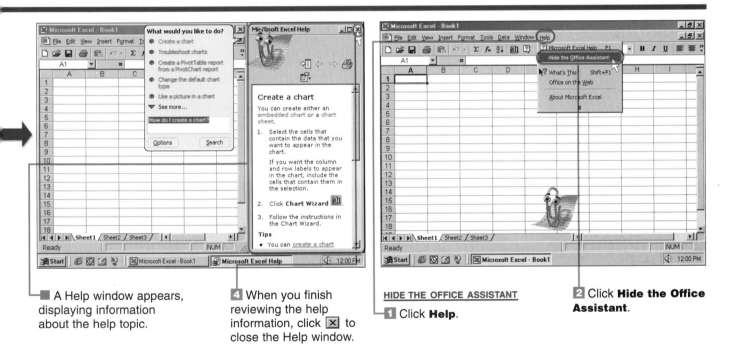

■ A Help window appears, displaying information about the help topic.

4 When you finish reviewing the help information, click ☒ to close the Help window.

HIDE THE OFFICE ASSISTANT

1 Click **Help**.

2 Click **Hide the Office Assistant**.

GETTING HELP

You can use Excel's
help index to locate
help topics of interest.

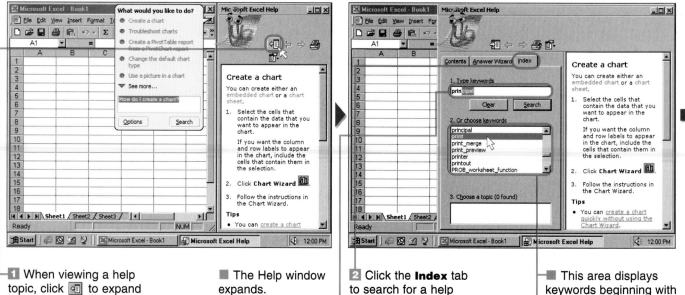

1 When viewing a help topic, click to expand the Help window.

Note: To view a help topic, perform steps 1 to 3 on page 22.

■ The Help window expands.

2 Click the **Index** tab to search for a help topic of interest.

3 Click this area and then type the first few letters of a topic of interest.

■ This area displays keywords beginning with the letters you typed.

4 Double-click a keyword of interest.

24

Why do some words in the Help window appear in blue?

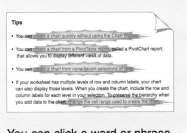

You can click a word or phrase that appears in blue without an underline to display a definition of the text. To hide the definition, click anywhere on your screen.

You can click a word or phrase that appears in blue with an underline to display a related help topic.

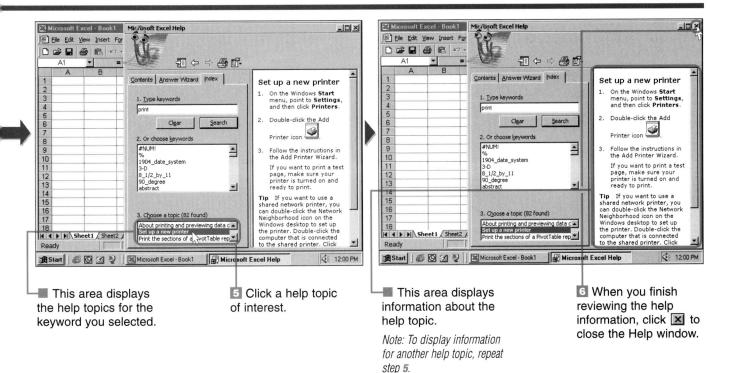

■ This area displays the help topics for the keyword you selected.

5 Click a help topic of interest.

■ This area displays information about the help topic.

Note: To display information for another help topic, repeat step 5.

6 When you finish reviewing the help information, click ☒ to close the Help window.

CHAPTER 2

Save and Open Your Workbooks

Are you wondering how to save, close or open an Excel workbook? Learn how in this chapter.

SAVE A WORKBOOK

You can save your workbook to store it for future use. This allows you to later review and make changes to the workbook.

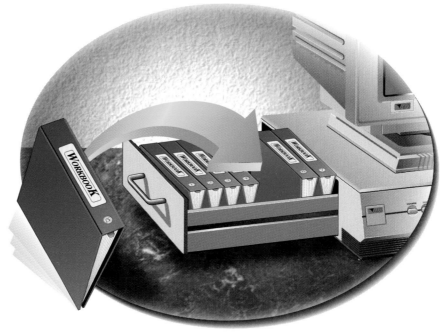

SAVE A WORKBOOK

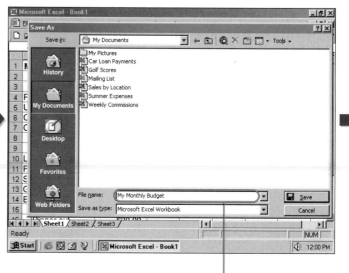

1 Click 🖫 to save your workbook.

Note: If 🖫 is not displayed, click 📄 on the Standard toolbar to display all the buttons.

■ The Save As dialog box appears.

Note: If you previously saved your workbook, the Save As dialog box will not appear since you have already named the workbook.

2 Type a name for the workbook.

What are the commonly used folders I can access?

History

Provides access to folders and workbooks you recently used.

My Documents

Provides a convenient place to store a workbook.

Desktop

Lets you store a workbook on the Windows desktop.

Favorites

Provides a place to store a workbook you will frequently access.

Web Folders

Can help you store a workbook on the Web.

■ This area shows the location where Excel will store your workbook. You can click this area to change the location.

■ This area allows you to access commonly used folders. To display the contents of a folder, click the folder.

3 Click **Save**.

■ Excel saves your workbook and displays the name of the workbook at the top of your screen.

SAVE CHANGES

You should regularly save changes you make to a workbook to avoid losing your work.

1 Click 🖫 to save changes you make to your workbook.

CREATE A NEW WORKBOOK

You can easily
create another
workbook to
store new data.

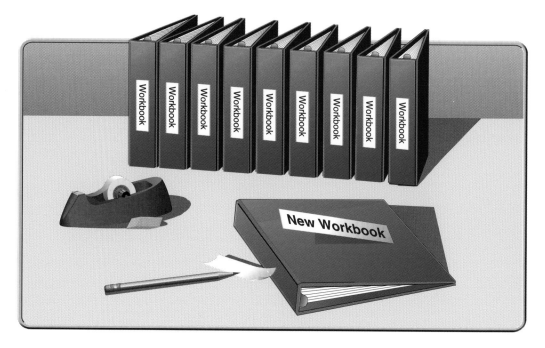

CREATE A NEW WORKBOOK

1 Click 🗋 to create
a new workbook.

*Note: If 🗋 is not displayed,
click 🔃 on the Standard toolbar
to display all the buttons.*

■ A new workbook
appears. The previous
workbook is now hidden
behind the new workbook.

■ A button for the new
workbook appears on
the taskbar.

Excel lets you have many workbooks open at once. You can easily switch from one open workbook to another.

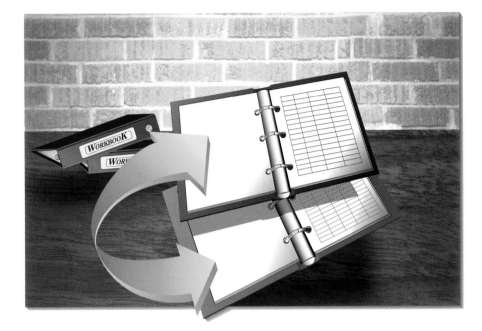

SWITCH BETWEEN WORKBOOKS

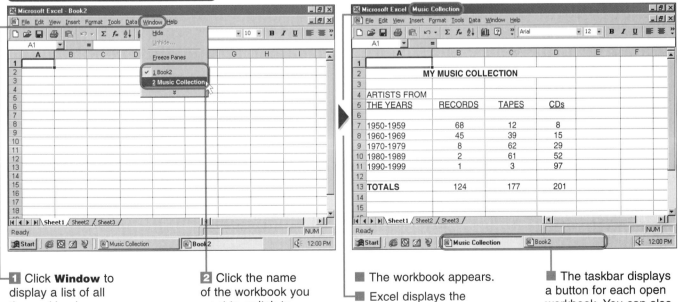

1 Click **Window** to display a list of all the workbooks you have open.

2 Click the name of the workbook you want to switch to.

■ The workbook appears.

■ Excel displays the name of the current workbook at the top of your screen.

■ The taskbar displays a button for each open workbook. You can also switch to a workbook by clicking its button on the taskbar.

VIEW ALL OPEN WORKBOOKS

If you have several workbooks open, some of them may be hidden from view. You can display the contents of all your open workbooks at once.

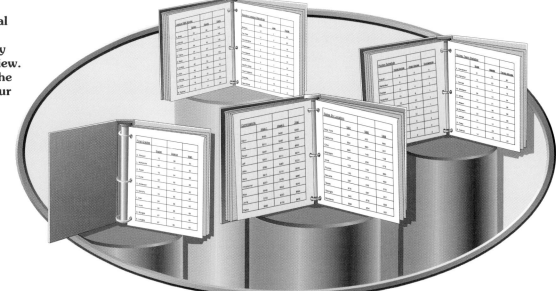

VIEW ALL OPEN WORKBOOKS

■1 Click **Window**.

■2 Click **Arrange**.

Note: If Arrange does not appear on the menu, position the mouse over the bottom of the menu to display all the menu commands.

■ The Arrange Windows dialog box appears.

■3 Click an option to select the way you want to arrange all your open workbooks (○ changes to ⊙).

■4 Click **OK** to arrange the workbooks.

How can I arrange open workbooks on my screen?

Tiled

Horizontal

Vertical

Cascade

■ You can now view the contents of all your open workbooks.

■ You can work with only one workbook at a time. The current workbook displays a blue title bar.

5 To make another workbook current, click anywhere in the workbook.

■ To once again maximize the current workbook to fill your screen, click ▣.

SAVE WORKBOOKS IN A WORKSPACE FILE

You can save related workbooks in a workspace file. Excel will remember the size and location of each workbook on your screen. You can later open the workspace file to open all the workbooks at once.

Before saving workbooks in a workspace file, save each workbook. To save a workbook, see page 28.

SAVE WORKBOOKS IN A WORKSPACE FILE

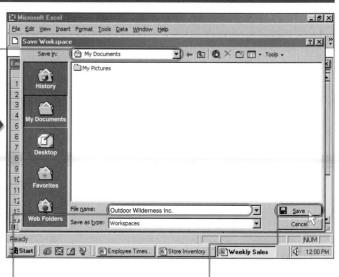

1 Display the workbooks you want to include in the workspace file. To arrange open workbooks, see page 32.

2 Click **File**.

3 Click **Save Workspace**.

Note: If Save Workspace does not appear on the menu, position the mouse ℕ over the bottom of the menu to display all the menu commands.

■ The Save Workspace dialog box appears.

4 Type a name for the workspace file.

■ This area shows the location where Excel will store your workspace file. You can click this area to change the location.

5 Click **Save**.

■ You can later open a workspace file as you would open any workbook. To open a workbook, see page 38.

SAVE A WORKBOOK WITH A NEW NAME

You can save a workbook with a different name. This is useful if you want to create a copy of the workbook that you can change.

SAVE A WORKBOOK WITH A NEW NAME

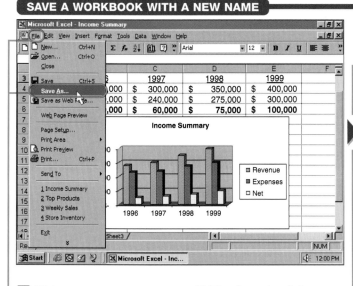

1 Click **File**.

2 Click **Save As**.

■ The Save As dialog box appears.

3 Type a name for the workbook.

■ This area shows the location where Excel will store your workbook. You can click this area to change the location.

4 Click **Save**.

■ Excel saves a copy of the workbook with the new name.

CLOSE A WORKBOOK

When you finish using a workbook, you can close the workbook to remove it from your screen.

When you close a workbook, you do not exit the Excel program. You can continue to work with other workbooks.

■ Save the workbook displayed on your screen before closing the workbook. To save a workbook, see page 28.

1 Click **File**.

2 Click **Close**.

■ The workbook disappears from your screen.

■ The button for the workbook disappears from the taskbar.

■ If you had more than one workbook open, the second last workbook you worked with appears on your screen.

When you finish
using Excel, you can
exit the program.

To prevent the loss of
data, you should always
exit all open programs
before turning off your
computer.

EXIT EXCEL

■ Save all open workbooks
before exiting Excel. To save
a workbook, see page 28.

1 Click **File**.

2 Click **Exit**.

■ The Microsoft Excel
window disappears from
your screen.

■ The button for the
program disappears
from the taskbar.

OPEN A WORKBOOK

You can open a saved
workbook and display
it on your screen. This
allows you to review
and make changes
to the workbook.

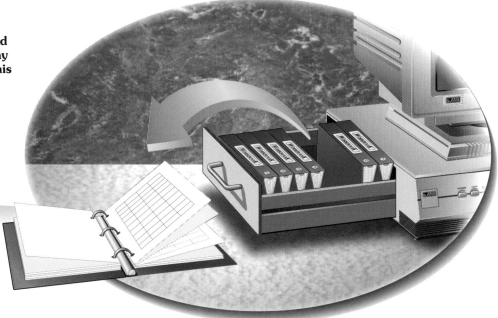

OPEN A WORKBOOK

1 Click 📂 to open
a workbook.

*Note: If 📂 is not displayed,
click 🔽 on the Standard toolbar
to display all the buttons.*

■ The Open dialog box
appears.

■ This area shows the
location of the displayed
workbooks. You can click
this area to change the
location.

■ This area allows you
to access commonly
used folders. To display
the contents of a folder,
click the folder.

*Note: For information on the
commonly used folders, see
the top of page 29.*

Can I quickly open a workbook I recently worked with?

Excel remembers the names of the last four workbooks you worked with. You can quickly open one of these workbooks.

■1 Click **File**.

■2 Click the name of the workbook you want to open.

Note: If the names of the last four workbooks you worked with are not all displayed, position the mouse over the bottom of the menu to display all the workbook names.

■2 Click the name of the workbook you want to open.

■3 Click **Open**.

■ Excel opens the workbook and displays it on your screen. You can now review and make changes to the workbook.

■ The name of the workbook appears at the top of your screen.

FIND A WORKBOOK

If you cannot remember
the name or location of
a workbook you want to
open, you can search for
the workbook.

Searching....

SALES SCHEDULE INVENTORY BUDGET

FIND A WORKBOOK

1 Click 📂 to display
the Open dialog box.

*Note: If 📂 is not displayed,
click ⏩ on the Standard toolbar
to display all the buttons.*

■ The Open dialog box
appears.

2 Click **Tools**.

3 Click **Find**.

■ The Find dialog box
appears.

How can I search for a workbook?

When searching for a workbook, you must specify a property for the search. Common properties include the worksheet contents, creation date and file name.

After you specify a property, you can specify a condition and value for the search.

-4 Click ▼ in this area to specify a property for the search.

-5 Click the property you want to use.

-6 Click ▼ in this area to specify a condition for the search.

-7 Click the condition you want to use.

Note: The available conditions depend on the property you selected in step 5.

-8 Click this area and type the value you want to search for.

Note: If the value area is not available, you do not need to enter a value.

CONTINUED

You can specify
the location where
you want to search
for a workbook.

9 Click ▼ in this area
to specify where you
want to search for the
workbook.

10 Click the location
you want to search.

11 To search the contents
of all the folders in the
location you specified,
click **Search subfolders**
(☐ changes to ☑).

12 Click **Add to List**
to confirm the search
criteria you specified.

■ The search criteria
you specified appears
in this area.

*Note: Excel automatically adds
the criteria **Files of type is All
Microsoft Excel Files** to the
list of search criteria for you.*

13 Click **Find Now** to
start the search.

?

When I started the search, why did a dialog box appear, asking if I want to install FindFast?

FindFast is a feature that can help speed up your searches. To install FindFast, insert the CD-ROM disc you used to install Excel into your CD-ROM drive. Then click **Yes** to install FindFast.

Microsoft Office ☓

ⓘ This operation would be considerably faster if FindFast were installed. Would you like to install FindFast now to speed this operation up in the future?

Yes   No

■ The Open dialog box reappears.

■ This area displays the names of the workbooks Excel found.

14 To open a workbook, click the name of the workbook.

15 Click **Open**.

■ Excel opens the workbook and displays it on your screen. You can now review and make changes to the workbook.

PROTECT A WORKBOOK

You can prevent other
people from opening
or making changes to a
workbook by protecting
it with a password.

You should save
a workbook before
protecting it with a
password. To save
a workbook, see
page 28.

page 28.

PROTECT A WORKBOOK

-1 Click **File**.

-2 Click **Save As**.

■ The Save As dialog
box appears.

-3 Click **Tools**.

-4 Click **General
Options**.

■ The Save Options
dialog box appears.

What password should I use to protect my workbook?

When choosing a password, you should not use words that people can easily associate with you, such as your name or favorite sport. The most effective passwords connect two words or numbers with a special character (example: **blue@123**). A password can contain up to 15 characters, including letters, numbers and symbols.

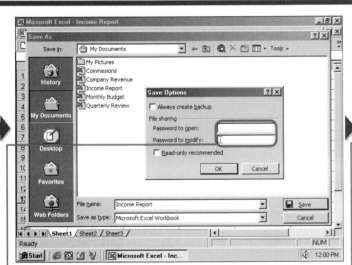

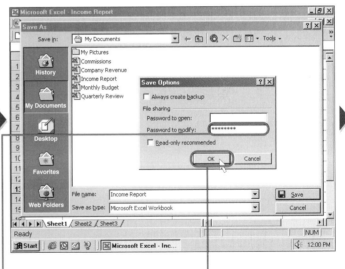

5 Click the box for the type of password you want to enter.

Password to open
Prevents people from opening the workbook without entering the correct password.

Password to modify
Prevents people from making changes to the workbook without entering the correct password.

6 Type the password you want to use.

7 Click **OK** to continue.

CONTINUED

PROTECT A WORKBOOK

After you protect
a workbook with
a password, Excel
will ask you to enter
the password each
time you open the
workbook.

You should write
down your password
and keep it in a safe
place. If you forget
the password, you
may not be able to
open the workbook.

PROTECT A WORKBOOK (CONTINUED)

■ The Confirm Password
dialog box appears, asking
you to confirm the password
you entered.

■8 Type the password again
to confirm the password.

■9 Click **OK**.

■10 Click **Save** in the
Save As dialog box.

■ A dialog box appears,
stating that you are about
to replace the existing file.

■11 Click **Yes** to replace the
file and save the workbook
with the password.

■ To unprotect a
workbook, perform steps **1**
to **7** starting on page 44,
except delete the existing
password in step **6**. Then
perform steps **10** and **11**.

? I typed the correct password, but Excel will not open my workbook. What is wrong?

Passwords in Excel are case sensitive. If you do not enter the correct uppercase and lowercase letters, Excel will not accept the password. For example, if your password is **Car**, you cannot enter **car** or **CAR** to open the workbook.

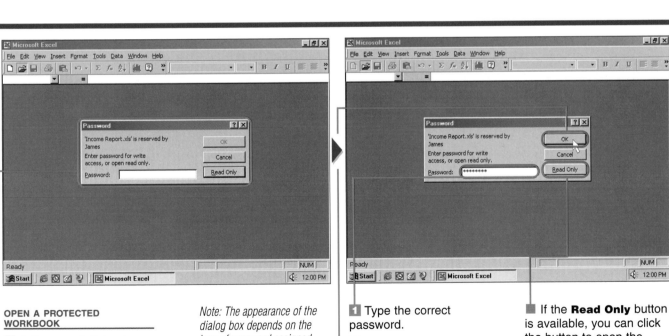

OPEN A PROTECTED WORKBOOK

■ A Password dialog box appears each time you open a protected workbook. To open a workbook, see page 38.

Note: The appearance of the dialog box depends on the type of password assigned to the workbook.

1 Type the correct password.

2 Click **OK**.

■ If the **Read Only** button is available, you can click the button to open the workbook without entering a password. You will not be able to save changes you make to the workbook.

CHAPTER 3

Edit Your Worksheets

Do you want to edit the data in your worksheet or check your worksheet for spelling errors? This chapter teaches you how.

EDIT DATA

You can edit data
in your worksheet
to correct a mistake
or update the data.

INCOME STATEMENT

Revenue	120,000	135,000	140,000
Payroll	35,000	35,000	35,000
Rent	15,000	15,000	15,000
Supplies	3,000	2,500	4,000
TOTAL EXPENSES			
Income			

EDIT DATA

1 Double-click the cell
containing the data you
want to edit.

■ A flashing insertion
point appears in the cell.

2 Press the ← or → key
to move the insertion point to
where you want to remove or
insert characters.

3 To remove the character to
the left of the insertion point,
press the ◆Backspace key.

■ To remove the
character to the right
of the insertion point,
press the Delete key.

50

How do I use the number keys on the right side of my keyboard to insert numbers?

When **NUM** appears at the bottom of your screen, you can use the number keys on the right side of your keyboard to insert numbers.

■ To turn the display of **NUM** on or off, press the `Num Lock` key.

REPLACE ALL DATA IN A CELL

4 To insert data where the insertion point flashes on your screen, type the data.

5 When you finish making changes to the data, press the `Enter` key.

1 Click the cell containing the data you want to replace with new data.

2 Type the new data and then press the `Enter` key.

DELETE DATA

You can remove data you no longer need from cells in your worksheet.

You can delete data from a single cell or from several cells at once.

DELETE DATA

1 Select the cells containing the data you want to delete. To select cells, see page 16.

2 Press the Delete key.

■ The data in the cells you selected disappears.

Excel remembers
the last changes
you made to your
worksheet. If you
regret these changes,
you can cancel them
by using the Undo
feature.

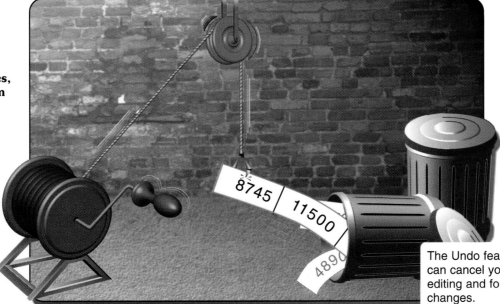

The Undo feature
can cancel your last
editing and formatting
changes.

UNDO CHANGES

1 Click 🔄 to undo the
last change you made
to your worksheet.

*Note: If 🔄 is not displayed,
click 🔽 on the Standard toolbar
to display all the buttons.*

■ Excel cancels the last
change you made to your
worksheet.

■ You can repeat step 1
to cancel previous
changes you made.

■ To reverse the
results of using the
Undo feature, click 🔁.

*Note: If 🔁 is not displayed,
click 🔽 on the Standard toolbar
to display all the buttons.*

MOVE OR COPY DATA

You can move or copy data to a new location in your worksheet by dragging and dropping the data. This method is useful when moving or copying data short distances in your worksheet.

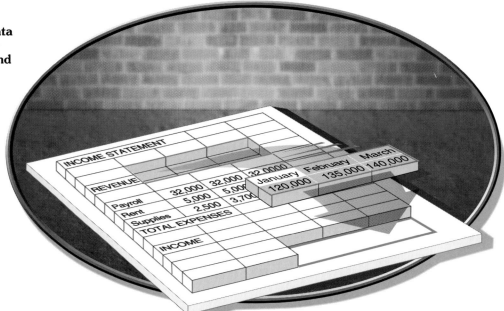

USING DRAG AND DROP

1 Select the cells containing the data you want to move or copy. To select cells, see page 16.

2 Position the mouse ⊕ over a border of the selected cells (⊕ changes to ⇖).

? What is the difference between moving and copying data?

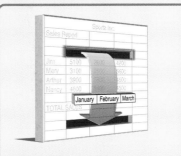

Moving data

Moving data allows you to reorganize data in your worksheet. When you move data, the data disappears from its original location in your worksheet.

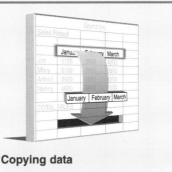

Copying data

Copying data allows you to repeat data in your worksheet without having to retype the data. When you copy data, the data appears in both the original and new locations.

3 To move the data, drag the mouse ⬚ to where you want to place the data.

■ To copy the data, press and hold down the **Ctrl** key as you drag the mouse ⬚ to where you want to place the data.

Note: A gray box indicates where the data will appear.

■ The data appears in the new location.

■ To immediately cancel the move or copy, click ⬚ .

Note: If ⬚ is not displayed, click ⬚ on the Standard toolbar to display all the buttons.

MOVE OR COPY DATA

You can move or copy data to a new location in your worksheet by using toolbar buttons. This method is useful when moving or copying data long distances in your worksheet.

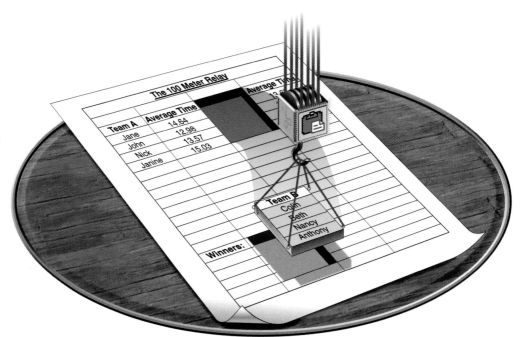

USING THE TOOLBAR BUTTONS

1 Select the cells containing the data you want to move or copy. To select cells, see page 16.

2 Click one of these buttons.

✂ Move data

📋 Copy data

Note: If the button you want is not displayed, click ⏩ on the Standard toolbar to display all the buttons.

3 Click the cell where you want to place the data. This cell will become the top left cell of the new location.

4 Click 📋 to place the data in the new location.

Note: If 📋 is not displayed, click ⏩ on the Standard toolbar to display all the buttons.

■ The data appears in the new location.

?

Can I use the Clipboard toolbar to move or copy a formula in my worksheet?

No. When you use the Clipboard toolbar to move or copy a formula in your worksheet, Excel places only the result of the formula in the new location. If you change the data used in the original formula, the result in the new location will not change. For information on formulas, see page 86.

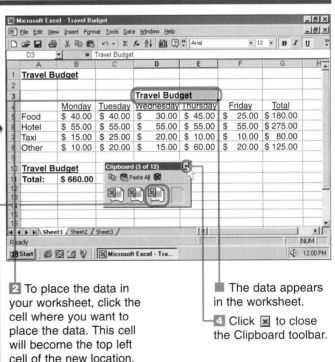

USING THE CLIPBOARD TOOLBAR

■ The Clipboard toolbar may appear when you move or copy data using the toolbar buttons. Each icon on the toolbar represents data you have selected to move or copy.

Note: To display the Clipboard toolbar, see page 118.

1 To see the data an icon represents, position the mouse over the icon. A yellow box appears, displaying the data.

2 To place the data in your worksheet, click the cell where you want to place the data. This cell will become the top left cell of the new location.

3 Click the icon to place the data in your worksheet.

■ The data appears in the worksheet.

4 Click **×** to close the Clipboard toolbar.

CHECK SPELLING

You can find and correct all the spelling errors in your worksheet.

Excel compares every word in your worksheet to words in its dictionary. If a word in your worksheet does not exist in the dictionary, Excel considers the word misspelled.

CHECK SPELLING

1 Click cell **A1** to start the spell check at the beginning of your worksheet.

2 Click 🔤 to start the spell check.

Note: If 🔤 is not displayed, click 📊 on the Standard toolbar to display all the buttons.

■ The Spelling dialog box appears if Excel finds a misspelled word.

■ This area displays the misspelled word.

■ This area displays suggestions for correcting the word.

Can Excel automatically correct my typing mistakes?

Excel automatically corrects many common spelling errors as you type.

adn	➡	and
alot	➡	a lot
comittee	➡	committee
don;t	➡	don't
nwe	➡	new
occurence	➡	occurrence
recieve	➡	receive
seperate	➡	separate
teh	➡	the

3 To select one of the suggestions, click the suggestion.

4 Click **Change** to correct the word in your worksheet.

■ To skip the word and continue checking your worksheet, click **Ignore**.

*Note: To skip the word and all occurrences of the word in your worksheet, click **Ignore All**.*

5 Correct or ignore misspelled words until this dialog box appears, telling you the spell check is complete.

6 Click **OK** to close the dialog box.

USING AUTOCORRECT

Excel automatically corrects hundreds of common typing and spelling errors as you type. You can create an AutoCorrect entry to add your own words and phrases to the list of errors that Excel corrects.

(c)	ⓒ
(tm)	TM
accordingto	according to
ahve	have
can;t	can't
chnage	change
may of been	may have been
recieve	receive
seperate	separate
teh	the

USING AUTOCORRECT

1 Click **Tools**.

2 Click **AutoCorrect**.

Note: If AutoCorrect does not appear on the menu, position the mouse ⟍ over the bottom of the menu to display all the menu commands.

■ The AutoCorrect dialog box appears.

■ This area displays the list of AutoCorrect entries included with Excel.

What types of AutoCorrect entries can I create?

You can create AutoCorrect entries for typing and spelling errors you often make. You can also create AutoCorrect entries to quickly enter words and phrases you frequently use, such as your name.

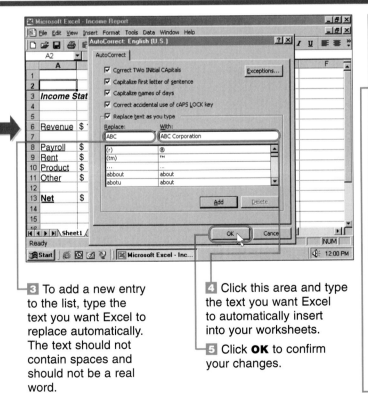

3 To add a new entry to the list, type the text you want Excel to replace automatically. The text should not contain spaces and should not be a real word.

4 Click this area and type the text you want Excel to automatically insert into your worksheets.

5 Click **OK** to confirm your changes.

INSERT AN AUTOCORRECT ENTRY

■ After you create an AutoCorrect entry, Excel will automatically insert the entry each time you type the corresponding text.

1 Click the cell where you want the AutoCorrect entry to appear.

2 Type the text Excel will automatically replace.

3 Press the **Enter** key and the AutoCorrect entry replaces the text you typed.

FIND DATA

You can use the Find feature to quickly locate a word or number in your worksheet.

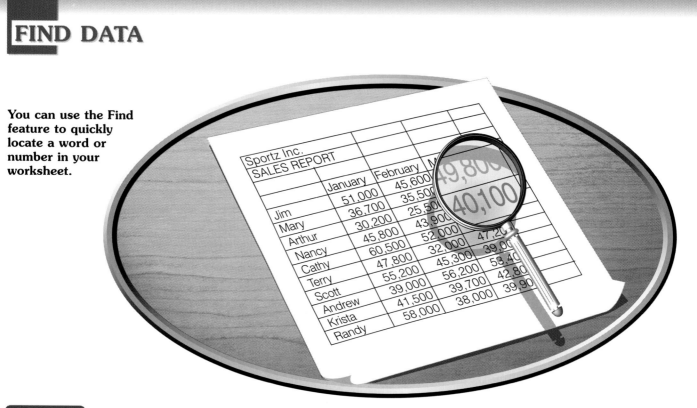

1 Click **Edit**.

2 Click **Find**.

■ The Find dialog box appears.

3 Type the word or number you want to find.

4 Click **Find Next** to start the search.

*Note: A dialog box appears if Excel cannot find the word or number you specified. Click **OK** to close the dialog box. Then skip to step 6.*

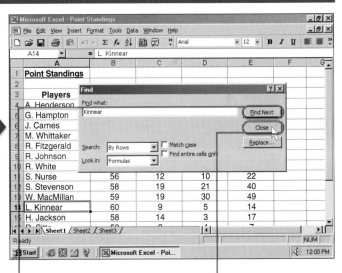

?

Can I search for part of a word or number?

When you search for data in your worksheet, Excel will find the data you specify even if the data is part of a larger word or number. For example, if you search for the number **105**, Excel will also find the numbers **105**.35, 2**105** and **105**6.

Find: 105

105.35 2**105** **105**6

■ Excel highlights the first cell containing the word or number.

■ To move the Find dialog box so you can clearly view the contents of the highlighted cell, position the mouse over the title bar and then drag the dialog box to a new location.

5 Click **Find Next** to find the next matching word or number. Repeat this step until you find the word or number you are searching for.

6 To close the Find dialog box at any time, click **Close**.

REPLACE DATA

The Replace feature can locate and replace every occurrence of a word or number in your worksheet. This is useful if you have incorrectly entered data throughout your worksheet.

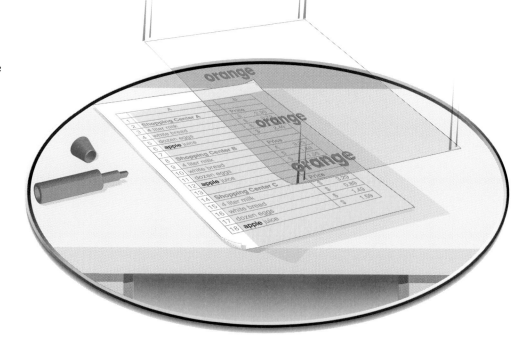

-1 Click **Edit**.

-2 Click **Replace**.

Note: If Replace does not appear on the menu, position the mouse over the bottom of the menu to display all the menu commands.

■ The Replace dialog box appears.

-3 Type the word or number you want to replace with new data.

-4 Press the **Tab** key and then type the new word or number.

-5 Click **Find Next** to start the search.

Can Excel find and replace a number used in my formulas?

Excel automatically searches the formulas in your worksheet for the number you specified. This is useful if you want to change a number used in several formulas. For example, if sales tax increases from 7% to 8%, you can search for all occurrences of **.07** in your formulas and replace them with **.08**.

Find what: .07
Replace with: .08

■ Excel highlights the first cell containing the word or number you specified.

6 Click one of these options.

Find Next - Ignore word or number

Replace - Replace word or number

Replace All - Replace all occurrences of word or number in the worksheet

7 Repeat step **6** until you find all the occurrences of the word or number you want to replace.

8 Click **Close** to close the Replace dialog box.

LINK DATA

You can link data in one cell to another cell. When you change the data in the original cell, the linked data will also display the changes.

Linking data is useful when you want cells to always display the same information.

LINK DATA

1 Click the cell containing the data you want to link to another cell.

2 Click 🖹 .

Note: If 🖹 is not displayed, click 🖹 on the Standard toolbar to display all the buttons.

3 Click the cell where you want to place the linked data.

Note: You can select a cell in the same worksheet, a worksheet in the same workbook or a worksheet in another workbook.

4 Click **Edit**.

5 Click **Paste Special**.

? **Can I move or delete the data in the original cell without affecting the link?**

When you move the data in the original cell, the link is not affected. When you delete the data in the original cell, the linked cell displays a zero (0).

■ The Paste Special dialog box appears.

6 Click **Paste Link**.

■ The linked data appears in the cell.

■ The formula bar displays the location of the original cell.

■ To remove the moving border around the original cell, press the **Esc** key.

■ When you change the data in the original cell, the linked data will also display the change.

CHANGE COLUMN WIDTH

You can improve
the appearance
of your worksheet
by changing the
width of columns.

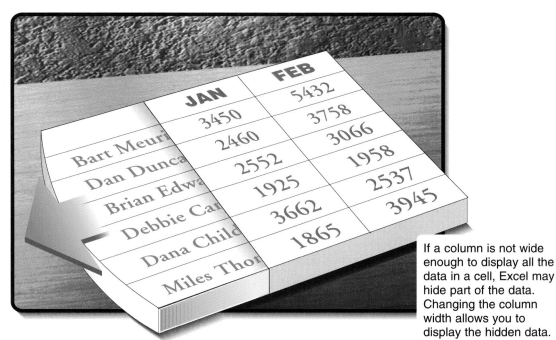

If a column is not wide
enough to display all the
data in a cell, Excel may
hide part of the data.
Changing the column
width allows you to
display the hidden data.

CHANGE COLUMN WIDTH

■1 To change the width
of a column, position the
mouse ⟡ over the right
edge of the column heading
(⟡ changes to ↔).

■2 Drag the column
edge until the dotted
line displays the column
width you want.

■ The column displays
the new width.

FIT LONGEST ITEM

■1 To change a column
width to fit the longest
item in the column,
double-click the right
edge of the column
heading.

You can change the height of rows to increase the space between the rows of data in your worksheet. This can help make the data easier to read.

CHANGE ROW HEIGHT

1 To change the height of a row, position the mouse 🖑 over the bottom edge of the row heading (🖑 changes to ✛).

2 Drag the row edge until the dotted line displays the row height you want.

■ The row displays the new height.

FIT TALLEST ITEM

1 To change a row height to fit the tallest item in the row, double-click the bottom edge of the row heading.

INSERT A ROW OR COLUMN

You can add a row or column to your worksheet when you want to insert additional data.

EMPLOYEE HOURS

	Week 1	Week 2	Week 3
Deb Shuter	45	32	37
Jen Wright	35	33	37
Dave Bibby	20	38	35
Jeff Evans	30	35	36
Sue Thomas	35	36	39
Julie Simak	37	38	41
Kevin Cooper	38	42	42

INSERT A ROW

Excel will insert a row above the row you select.

1 To select a row, click the row number.

2 Click **Insert**.

3 Click **Rows**.

■ The new row appears and all the rows that follow shift downward.

How do I insert several rows or columns at once?

You can use the method shown below to insert several rows or columns at once, but you must first select the number of rows or columns you want to insert. For example, to insert three rows, select three rows before performing steps **2** and **3** on page 70.

Note: To select rows or columns, see page 16.

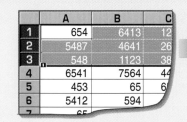

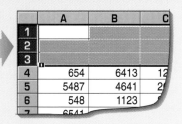

INSERT A COLUMN

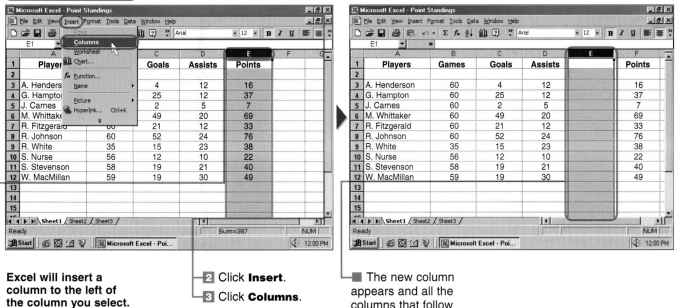

Excel will insert a column to the left of the column you select.

1 To select a column, click the column letter.

2 Click **Insert**.

3 Click **Columns**.

■ The new column appears and all the columns that follow shift to the right.

DELETE A ROW OR COLUMN

You can delete a row or column from your worksheet to remove data you no longer need.

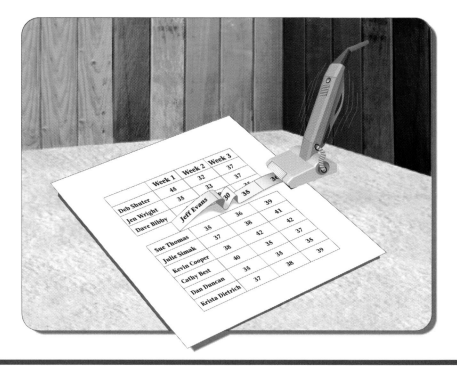

1 To select the row you want to delete, click the row number.

2 Click **Edit**.

3 Click **Delete**.

■ The row disappears and all the rows that follow shift upward.

■ To immediately return the row to the worksheet, click ↶ .

Note: If ↶ is not displayed, click ⬧ on the Standard toolbar to display all the buttons.

?

How do I delete several rows or columns at once?

Press and hold down the `Ctrl` key as you click the numbers of the rows or letters of the columns you want to delete. Then perform steps **2** and **3** below.

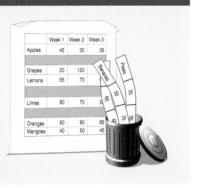

DELETE A COLUMN

1 To select the column you want to delete, click the column letter.

2 Click **Edit**.

3 Click **Delete**.

■ The column disappears and all the columns that follow shift to the left.

■ To immediately return the column to the worksheet, click 🔄.

Note: If 🔄 is not displayed, click 🔧 on the Standard toolbar to display all the buttons.

INSERT CELLS

If you want to add new data to the middle of existing data, you can insert cells. The surrounding cells move to make room for the new cells.

Car Expenses		
	Janua	$ 102.00
Car Loan	$ 451.00	$ 451.00
Fuel		$ 89.00
	$ 177.00	$ 177.00
Insurance	$ 75.00	$ 177.00
Parking	$ 356.12	$ 68.00
Maintenance	$ 12.50	$ 32.89
Miscellaneous		$ 42.39

INSERT CELLS

1 Select the cells where you want to insert new cells. To select cells, see page 16.

Note: Excel will insert the same number of cells as you select.

2 Click **Insert**.

3 Click **Cells**.

Note: If Cells does not appear on the menu, position the mouse Ⓚ over the bottom of the menu to display all the menu commands.

■ The Insert dialog box appears.

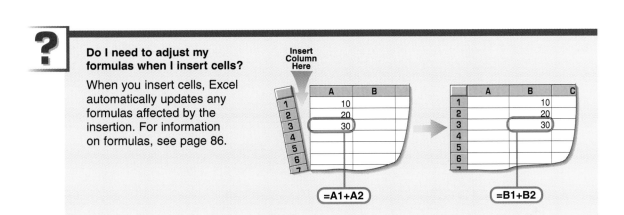

Do I need to adjust my formulas when I insert cells?

When you insert cells, Excel automatically updates any formulas affected by the insertion. For information on formulas, see page 86.

4 Click an option to shift the surrounding cells to the right or downward to make room for the new cells (○ changes to ⊙).

5 Click **OK** to insert the cells.

■ Excel inserts the new cells and shifts the surrounding cells in the direction you specified.

DELETE CELLS

You can remove cells you no longer need from your worksheet. The surrounding cells move to fill the empty space.

	Expenses	Profit
$ 245,000	$ 203,345	$ 41,655
$ 245,995		
$ 250,000	$ 199,900	$ 75,990
$ 275,890	$ 210,700	$ 28,400
$ 239,100	$ 210,445	$ 10,540
$ 220,985	$ 207,600	$ 6,190
$ 213,790	$ 209,200	$ 26,470
$ 235,670		

$ 209,560 $ 36,435
00,480 $ 49,520

---

1 Select the cells you want to delete. To select cells, see page 16.

2 Click **Edit**.

3 Click **Delete**.

■ The Delete dialog box appears.

Why did #REF! appear in a cell after I deleted cells in my worksheet?

If **#REF!** appears in a cell in your worksheet, you deleted data needed to calculate a formula. Before deleting cells, make sure the cells do not contain data that is used in a formula. For information on formulas, see page 86.

■ **4** Click an option to shift the surrounding cells to the left or upward to fill the empty space (○ changes to ◉).

5 Click **OK** to delete the cells.

■ Excel removes the cells and shifts the surrounding cells in the direction you specified.

■ To immediately return the cells to the worksheet, click 🔄 .

Note: If 🔄 is not displayed, click 🔽 on the Standard toolbar to display all the buttons.

NAME CELLS

You can give cells in your worksheet a meaningful name. Using named cells can save you time when selecting cells or entering formulas.

You can name a single cell or a range of cells in your worksheet.

NAME CELLS

1 Select the cells you want to name. To select cells, see page 16.

2 Click this area to highlight the existing information.

3 Type the name you want to use for the cells. The name cannot start with a number or contain spaces.

4 Press the `Enter` key to name the cells.

How can naming cells help me enter formulas?

Naming cells can make formulas easier to enter and understand.

■ This cell contains the formula **=Income-Expenses** instead of the formula **=B3-C3**.

Note: For information on formulas, see page 86.

■ This cell was named **Income**.

■ This cell was named **Expenses**.

SELECT NAMED CELLS

1 Click ▼ in this area.

2 Click the name of the cells you want to select.

■ Excel highlights the cells in your worksheet.

You can add a comment to a cell in your worksheet. A comment can provide a note, explanation or reminder about data you need to verify later.

ADD A COMMENT

1 Click the cell you want to add a comment to.

2 Click **Insert**.

3 Click **Comment**.

Note: If Comment does not appear on the menu, position the mouse ⩩ over the bottom of the menu to display all the menu commands.

■ A yellow comment box appears, displaying your name.

4 Type the comment you want to add.

5 When you finish typing your comment, click outside the comment box.

How can I display all the comments in my worksheet at once?

View

☐ Normal
☐ Page Break Preview

Toolbars ▶

✓ Formula Bar
✓ Status Bar

Header and Footer...
☐ **Comments**

Custom Views...
☐ Full Screen

Zoom...

1 Click **View**.

2 Click **Comments**.

Note: If Comments does not appear on the menu, position the mouse ⬚ over the bottom of the menu to display all the menu commands.

■ To once again hide the comments, repeat steps **1** and **2**.

■ A red triangle (◥) appears in the cell to indicate that the cell contains a comment.

DISPLAY A COMMENT

1 Position the mouse ⬚ over the cell containing the comment you want to view.

■ The comment box appears, displaying the comment.

2 To hide the comment, move the mouse ⬚ outside the cell.

You can edit a comment to update the information it displays. You can also delete a comment you no longer need.

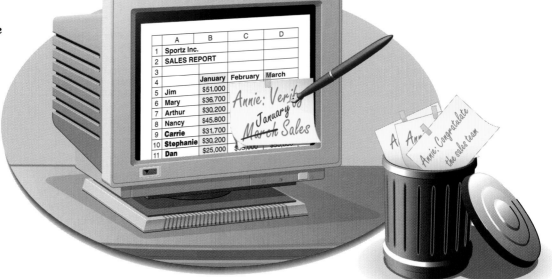

EDIT A COMMENT

1 Click the cell containing the comment you want to edit.

2 Click **Insert**.

3 Click **Edit Comment**.

Note: If Edit Comment does not appear on the menu, position the mouse ▷ over the bottom of the menu to display all the menu commands.

■ The comment box appears. You can now edit the comment.

4 When you finish editing the comment, click outside the comment box.

? Why didn't my comments print when I printed my worksheet?

You must change Excel's print options to specify that you want to print your comments. To change the print options, see page 178.

You can choose to print the comments on a separate page or as they are displayed in your worksheet. To print the comments as they are displayed in your worksheet, you must first display all the comments. To display all the comments, see the top of page 81.

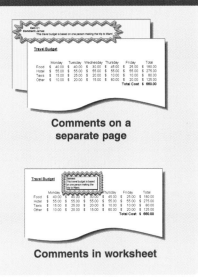

Comments on a separate page

Comments in worksheet

DELETE A COMMENT

1 Click the cell containing the comment you want to delete.

2 Click **Edit**.

3 Click **Clear**.

4 Click **Comments**.

■ The red triangle (◣) disappears from the cell.

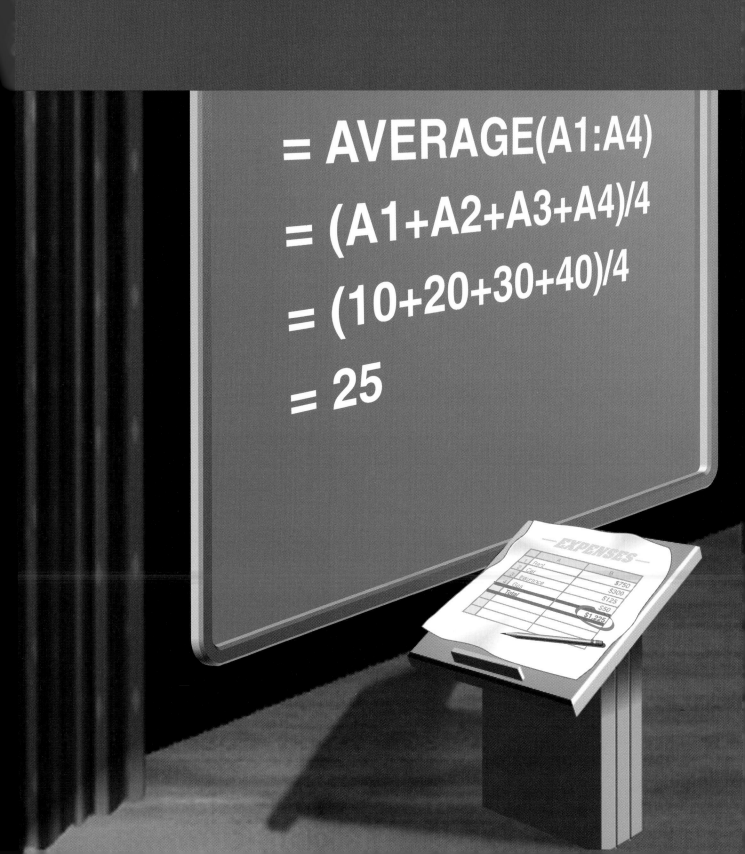

CHAPTER 4

Work With Formulas and Functions

Would you like to perform calculations on the data in your worksheet? Learn how in this chapter.

INTRODUCTION TO FORMULAS

A formula allows you to calculate and analyze data in your worksheet.

A formula always begins with an equal sign (=).

INTRODUCTION TO FORMULAS

$$45 - 3 + 4 * 5 = 62$$

OR

$$45 - (3 + 4) * 5 = 10$$

Order of Calculations

Excel performs calculations in the following order:

1 Exponents (^)

2 Multiplication (*) and Division (/)

3 Addition (+) and Subtraction (-)

You can use parentheses ( ) to change the order in which Excel performs calculations. Excel will perform the calculations inside the parentheses first.

Cell References

When entering formulas, use cell references instead of actual data whenever possible. For example, enter the formula **=A1+A2** instead of **=10+30**.

When you use cell references and you change a number used in a formula, Excel will automatically redo the calculation for you.

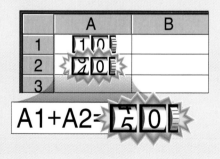

EXAMPLES OF FORMULAS

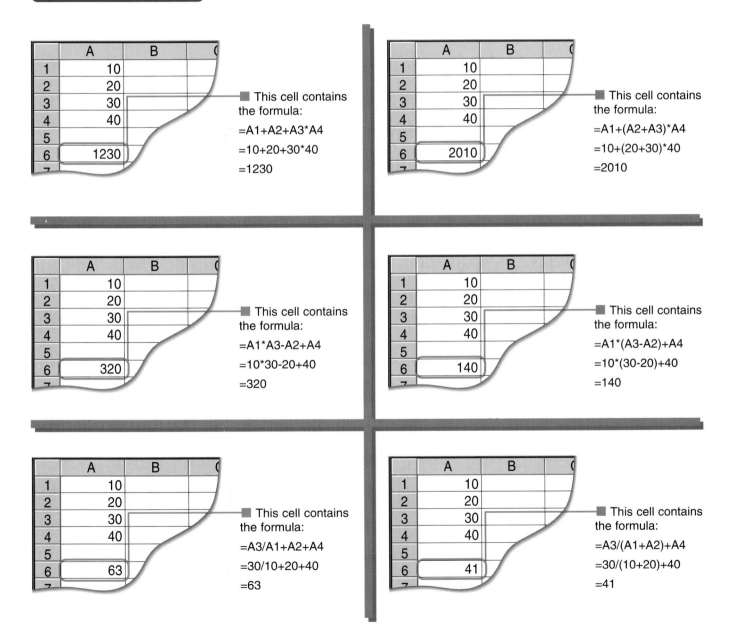

	A	B	C
1	10		
2	20		
3	30		
4	40		
5			
6	1230		
7			

■ This cell contains the formula:

=A1+A2+A3*A4

=10+20+30*40

=1230

	A	B	C
1	10		
2	20		
3	30		
4	40		
5			
6	2010		
7			

■ This cell contains the formula:

=A1+(A2+A3)*A4

=10+(20+30)*40

=2010

	A	B	C
1	10		
2	20		
3	30		
4	40		
5			
6	320		
7			

■ This cell contains the formula:

=A1*A3-A2+A4

=10*30-20+40

=320

	A	B	C
1	10		
2	20		
3	30		
4	40		
5			
6	140		
7			

■ This cell contains the formula:

=A1*(A3-A2)+A4

=10*(30-20)+40

=140

	A	B	C
1	10		
2	20		
3	30		
4	40		
5			
6	63		
7			

■ This cell contains the formula:

=A3/A1+A2+A4

=30/10+20+40

=63

	A	B	C
1	10		
2	20		
3	30		
4	40		
5			
6	41		
7			

■ This cell contains the formula:

=A3/(A1+A2)+A4

=30/(10+20)+40

=41

ENTER A FORMULA

You can enter a formula into any cell in your worksheet. A formula helps you calculate and analyze data in your worksheet.

1 Click the cell where you want to enter a formula.

2 Type an equal sign (=) to begin the formula.

3 Type the formula and then press the **Enter** key.

■ The result of the calculation appears in the cell.

4 To view the formula you entered, click the cell containing the formula.

■ The formula for the cell appears in the formula bar.

? **What happens if I change a number used in a formula?**

If you change a number used in a formula, Excel will automatically redo the calculation for you.

	A	B
1	Rent	750
2	Car	300
3	Insurance	125
4	Gas	*100* ~~50~~
5	Total	*1,275* ~~1,225~~

1275

EDIT A FORMULA

1 Double-click the cell containing the formula you want to change.

■ The formula appears in the cell.

■ Excel uses different colors to outline each cell used in the formula.

2 Press the ← or → key to move the flashing insertion point to where you want to remove or add characters.

3 To remove the character to the left of the insertion point, press the ◆Backspace key.

4 To add data where the insertion point flashes on your screen, type the data.

5 When you finish making changes to the formula, press the Enter key.

INTRODUCTION TO FUNCTIONS

A function is a ready-to-use formula that you can use to perform a calculation on the data in your worksheet.

INTRODUCTION TO FUNCTIONS

■ A function always begins with an equal sign (=).

■ The data Excel will use to calculate a function is enclosed in parentheses ( ).

```
=SUM(A1,A2,A3)

=AVERAGE(C1,C2,C3)

=MAX(B7,C7,D7,E7)

=COUNT(D12,D13,D14)
```

```
=SUM(A1:A3)

=AVERAGE(C1:C3)

=MAX(B7:E7)

=COUNT(D12:D14)
```

Specify Individual Cells

When a comma (,) separates cell references in a function, Excel uses each cell to perform the calculation.

For example, =SUM(A1,A2,A3) is the same as the formula =A1+A2+A3.

Specify Group of Cells

When a colon (:) separates cell references in a function, Excel uses the specified cells and all cells between them to perform the calculation.

For example, =SUM(A1:A3) is the same as the formula =A1+A2+A3.

COMMON FUNCTIONS

Average

Calculates the average value of a list of numbers.

	A	B
1	10	
2	20	
3	30	
4	40	
5		
6	25	

■ This cell contains the function:

=AVERAGE(A1:A4)

=(A1+A2+A3+A4)/4

=(10+20+30+40)/4

=25

Count

Calculates the number of values in a list.

	A	B
1	10	
2	20	
3	30	
4	40	
5		
6	4	

■ This cell contains the function:

=COUNT(A1:A4)

=4

Max

Finds the largest value in a list of numbers.

	A	B
1	10	
2	20	
3	30	
4	40	
5		
6	40	

■ This cell contains the function:

=MAX(A1:A4)

=40

Min

Finds the smallest value in a list of numbers.

	A	B
1	10	
2	20	
3	30	
4	40	
5		
6	10	

■ This cell contains the function:

=MIN(A1:A4)

=10

Sum

Adds a list of numbers.

	A	B
1	10	
2	20	
3	30	
4	40	
5		
6	100	

■ This cell contains the function:

=SUM(A1:A4)

=A1+A2+A3+A4

=10+20+30+40

=100

Round

Rounds a value to a specific number of digits.

	A	B
1	42.3617	
2		
3		
4		
5		
6	42.36	

■ This cell contains the function:

=ROUND(A1,2)

=42.36

ENTER A FUNCTION

Excel helps you enter functions in your worksheet. Functions let you perform calculations without typing long, complex formulas.

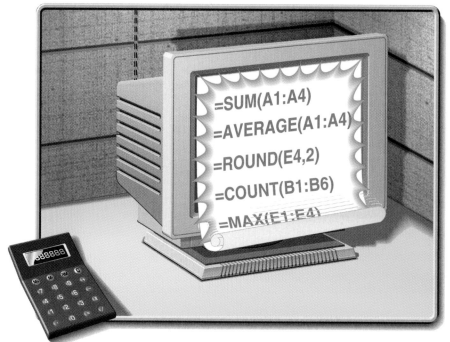

=SUM(A1:A4)
=AVERAGE(A1:A4)
=ROUND(E4,2)
=COUNT(B1:B6)
=MAX(E1:E4)

ENTER A FUNCTION

1 Click the cell where you want to enter a function.

2 Click f_* to enter a function.

Note: If f_* is not displayed, click ➥ on the Standard toolbar to display all the buttons.

■ The Paste Function dialog box appears.

3 Click the category containing the function you want to use.

*Note: If you do not know which category contains the function you want to use, select **All** to display a list of all the functions.*

■ This area displays the functions in the category you selected.

4 Click the function you want to use.

How many functions does Excel offer?

Excel offers over 200 functions to help you analyze data in your worksheet. There are financial functions, math and trigonometry functions, date and time functions, statistical functions and many more.

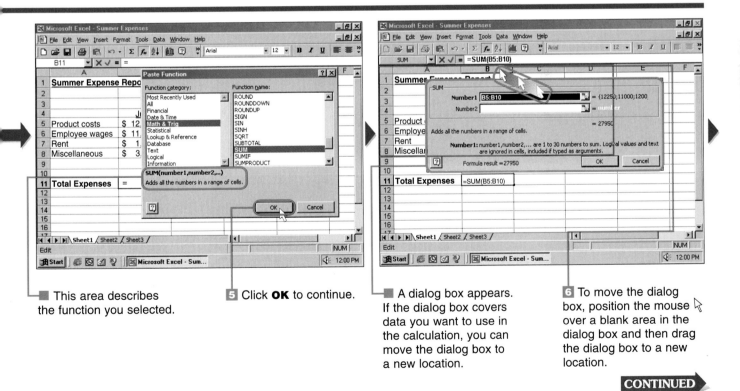

■ This area describes the function you selected.

5 Click **OK** to continue.

■ A dialog box appears. If the dialog box covers data you want to use in the calculation, you can move the dialog box to a new location.

6 To move the dialog box, position the mouse over a blank area in the dialog box and then drag the dialog box to a new location.

CONTINUED

ENTER A FUNCTION

When entering a function, you must specify which numbers you want to use in the calculation.

ENTER A FUNCTION (CONTINUED)

■ This area displays boxes where you enter the numbers you want to use in the calculation.

■ This area describes the numbers you need to enter.

7 To enter a number for the function, click the cell that contains the number.

Note: If the number you want to use does not appear in your worksheet, type the number.

■ The cell reference for the number appears in this area.

? Can I enter a function myself?

If you know the name of the
function you want to use, you
can type the function and cell
references directly into a cell
in your worksheet.

8 Click the next box to
enter the next number.

9 Repeat steps **7** and **8**
until you have entered all
the numbers you want to
use in the calculation.

10 Click **OK** to enter
the function in your
worksheet.

■ The result of the
function appears in
the cell.

■ The function for the cell
appears in the formula bar.

USING AUTOCALCULATE

You can view the
results of common
calculations without
entering a formula
into your worksheet.

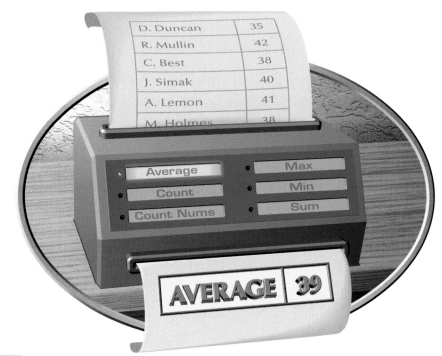

1 Select the cells you
want to include in the
calculation. To select
cells, see page 16.

■ This area displays
the sum of the cells
you selected.

2 To display the result
for a different calculation,
right-click this area.

? What calculations can I perform using AutoCalculate?

Average

Calculates the average value of a list of numbers.

Count

Calculates the number of items in a list, including text.

Count Nums

Calculates the number of values in a list.

Max

Finds the largest value in a list.

Min

Finds the smallest value in a list.

Sum

Adds a list of numbers.

■ A list appears, displaying the calculations you can perform.

3 Click the calculation you want to perform.

■ This area displays the result for the new calculation.

You can calculate the sum of a list of numbers in your worksheet.

1 Click the cell below or to the right of the cells containing the numbers you want to add.

2 Click Σ to add the numbers.

Note: If Σ is not displayed, click » on the Standard toolbar to display all the buttons.

■ Excel outlines the cells it will use in the calculation with a dotted line.

■ If Excel does not outline the correct cells, select the cells containing the numbers you want to add. To select cells, see page 16.

?

How do I calculate the sum of rows and columns of data at the same time?

1 Select the cells containing the numbers you want to add and a blank row and column for the results. To select cells, see page 16.

2 Click Σ to perform the calculations.

	Product A	Product B	Month Totals
January	10	5	
February	20	6	
Product Totals			

	Product A	Product B	Month Totals
January	10	5	15
February	20	6	26
Product Totals	30	11	41

Microsoft Excel - Weekly Sales

File Edit View Insert Format Tools Data Window Help

B10

	A	B	C	D	E	F
1	Sales					
2						
3		Week 1	Week 2	Week 3		
4	Tim	$2,000.00	$2,200.00	$2,100.00		
5	Michael	$1,500.00	$1,750.00	$1,850.00		
6	Monica	$1,750.00	$1,500.00	$1,850.00		
7	Jerry	$2,100.00	$2,000.00	$2,200.00		
8	Laurie	$1,800.00	$1,600.00	$2,000.00		
9	Total Sales:	$9,150.00				
10						
11						
12						
13						
14						
15						

Sheet1 / Sheet2 / Sheet3 /

Ready NUM

Start Microsoft Excel - We... 12:00 PM

3 Press the **Enter** key to perform the calculation.

■ The result of the calculation appears.

Microsoft Excel - Sales

File Edit View Insert Format Tools Data Window Help

SUM =SUM(C11,C8,C5)

	A	B	C	D	E	F
1						
2	Product	Salesperson	Units Sold			
3	T-shirts	Sue	326			
4	T-shirts	Patrick	289			
5	T-shirts Total		615			
6	Caps	Sue	493			
7	Caps	Patrick	507			
8	Caps Total		1000			
9	Shorts	Sue	316			
10	Shorts	Patrick	349			
11	Shorts Total		665			
12	Grand Total:		=SUM(C11,C8,C5)			
13						
14						
15						

Sheet1 / Sheet2 / Sheet3 /

Point NUM

Start Microsoft Excel - Sales 12:00 PM

CALCULATE A GRAND TOTAL

If your worksheet contains several subtotals, you can calculate a grand total.

■ These cells contain subtotals.

1 Click the cell below or to the right of the cells containing the subtotals.

2 Click Σ.

Note: If Σ is not displayed, click on the Standard toolbar to display all the buttons.

3 Press the **Enter** key to perform the calculation.

COPY A FORMULA

If you want to use the same formula several times in your worksheet, you can save time by copying the formula.

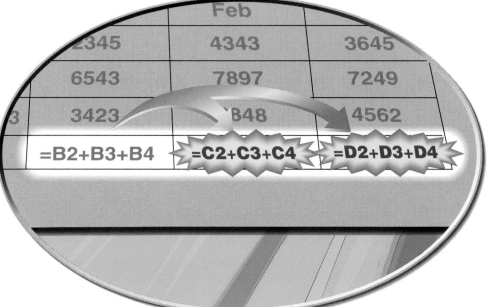

Feb		
2345	4343	3645
6543	7897	7249
3423	848	4562
=B2+B3+B4	=C2+C3+C4	=D2+D3+D4

COPY A FORMULA—USING RELATIVE REFERENCES

1 Enter the formula you want to copy to other cells. To enter a formula, see page 88.

*Note: In this example, cell **B10** contains the formula =B5+B6+B7+B8.*

2 Click the cell containing the formula you want to copy.

3 Position the mouse ⇩ over the bottom right corner of the cell (⇩ changes to **+**).

4 Drag the mouse **+** over the cells you want to receive a copy of the formula.

What is a relative reference?

A relative reference is a cell reference that changes when you copy a formula.

	A	B	C
1	10	20	5
2	20	30	10
3	30	40	20
4	60	90	35
5			

=A1+A2+A3 ➡ =B1+B2+B3   =C1+C2+C3

This cell contains the formula **=A1+A2+A3**.

If you copy the formula to other cells in your worksheet, Excel automatically changes the cell references in the new formulas.

■ The results of the formulas appear.

5 To see one of the new formulas, click a cell that received a copy of the formula.

■ The formula bar displays the formula with the new cell references.

COPY A FORMULA

You can copy a formula to other cells in your worksheet to save time. If you do not want Excel to change a cell reference when you copy a formula, you can use an absolute reference.

	A	B	C	D
1		R. Brown	J. Smith	K. Turner
2	Sales	100	200	300
3				
4	Commission	=$A$7*B2	=$A$7*C2	=$A$7*D2
5				
6	Commission Rate			
7	0.2			

COPY A FORMULA—USING ABSOLUTE REFERENCES

1 Enter the data you want to use in all the formulas.

2 Enter the formula you want to copy to other cells. To enter a formula, see page 88.

*Note: In this example, cell C4 contains the formula =$B$7*B4.*

3 Click the cell containing the formula you want to copy.

4 Position the mouse ⇩ over the bottom right corner of the cell (⇩ changes to +).

5 Drag the mouse + over the cells you want to receive a copy of the formula.

102

What is an absolute reference?

An absolute reference is a cell reference that does not change when you copy a formula. To make a cell reference absolute, type a dollar sign (**$**) before both the column letter and row number, such as **$A$7**.

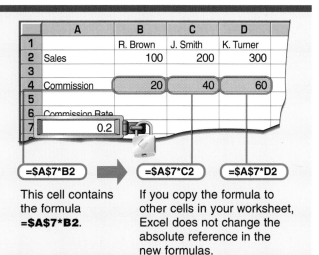

	A	B	C	D
1		R. Brown	J. Smith	K. Turner
2	Sales	100	200	300
3				
4	Commission	20	40	60
5				
6	Commission Rate			
7	0.2			

=$A$7*B2   →   =$A$7*C2   =$A$7*D2

This cell contains the formula **=$A$7*B2**.

If you copy the formula to other cells in your worksheet, Excel does not change the absolute reference in the new formulas.

Microsoft Excel - Grocery Bill

C4   = =$B$1*B4

	A	B	C
1	Sales Tax=	0.07	
2			
3		Price	Tax
4	Eggs	$ 0.99	$ 0.07
5	Bread	$ 1.19	$ 0.08
6	Ground Beef	$ 2.99	$ 0.21
7	Tuna (4 cans)	$ 4.24	$ 0.30
8	Milk	$ 2.29	$ 0.16
9	Cereal	$ 2.19	$ 0.15
10	Potatoes	$ 2.99	$ 0.21
11	Oranges	$ 3.25	$ 0.23
12	Chicken Breasts	$ 9.99	$ 0.70
13	Total	$ 30.12	$ 2.11

Sum= $ 4.22   NUM

■ The results of the formulas appear.

Microsoft Excel - Grocery Bill

C13   = =$B$1*B13

	A	B	C
1	Sales Tax=	0.07	
2			
3		Price	Tax
4	Eggs	$ 0.99	$ 0.07
5	Bread	$ 1.19	$ 0.08
6	Ground Beef	$ 2.99	$ 0.21
7	Tuna (4 cans)	$ 4.24	$ 0.30
8	Milk	$ 2.29	$ 0.16
9	Cereal	$ 2.19	$ 0.15
10	Potatoes	$ 2.99	$ 0.21
11	Oranges	$ 3.25	$ 0.23
12	Chicken Breasts	$ 9.99	$ 0.70
13	Total	$ 30.12	$ 2.11

6 To see one of the new formulas, click a cell that received a copy of the formula.

■ The formula bar displays the formula with the new cell references.

■ The absolute reference (**$B$1**) in the formula did not change. The relative reference (**B13**) in the formula did change.

DISPLAY FORMULAS

You can display the
formulas in your worksheet
instead of the results of
your calculations. This
is useful when you want
to review or edit all the
formulas in your worksheet.

Sales

	A	B	C	D
		Week 1	Week 2	Total
1		$ 2,000	$ 2,200	=B2+C2
2	Tim	$ 1,500	$ 1,750	=B3+C3
3	Michael	$ 1,750	$ 1,500	=B4+C4
4	Monica	$ 2,100	$ 2,000	=B5+C5
5	Jerry	$ 1,800	$ 1,600	=B6+C6
6	Laurie	$ 1,250	$ 1,500	=B7+C7
7	Roger	$ 2,100	$ 2,300	=B8+C8
8	Mike	$ 1,950	$ 2,150	=B9+C9
9	Lisa	$ 1,350	$ 1,650	=B10+C10
10	Pat	$ 1,250	$ 1,6	=B11+C11
11	June			

DISPLAY FORMULAS

■ This cell contains a
formula. By default, Excel
displays formula results
in your worksheet.

■ The formula bar
displays the formula
for the active cell.

1 To display the
formulas in your
worksheet, click **Tools**.

2 Click **Options**.

■ The Options dialog
box appears.

Is there another way to display the formulas in my worksheet?

You can use the keyboard to switch between the display of formulas and formula results in your worksheet. To change the display at any time, press and hold down the **Ctrl** key as you press the ~ key.

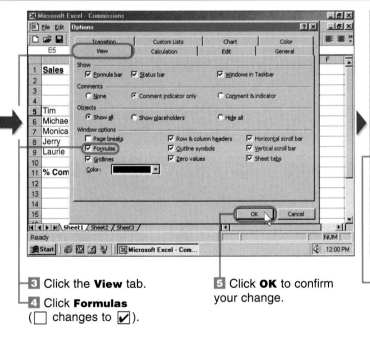

3 Click the **View** tab.

4 Click **Formulas** (☐ changes to ☑).

5 Click **OK** to confirm your change.

■ The formulas appear in your worksheet.

■ Excel automatically adjusts the widths of the columns in your worksheet to clearly display the formulas. To change the width of columns yourself, see page 68.

■ To once again show the formula results in your worksheet, repeat steps **1** to **5** (☑ changes to ☐ in step **4**).

ERRORS IN FORMULAS

An error message appears when Excel cannot properly calculate or display the result of a formula.

Errors in formulas are often the result of typing mistakes. You can correct an error by editing the formula. To edit a formula, see page 89.

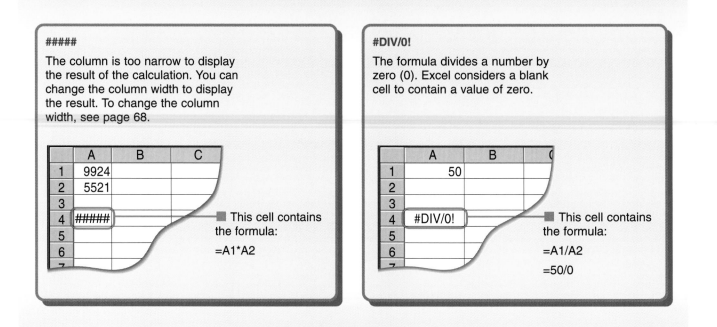

The column is too narrow to display the result of the calculation. You can change the column width to display the result. To change the column width, see page 68.

	A	B	C
1	9924		
2	5521		
3			
4	#####		
5			
6			
7			

■ This cell contains the formula:

=A1*A2

#DIV/0!

The formula divides a number by zero (0). Excel considers a blank cell to contain a value of zero.

	A	B	C
1	50		
2			
3			
4	#DIV/0!		
5			
6			
7			

■ This cell contains the formula:

=A1/A2

=50/0

#NAME?

The formula contains a function name or cell reference Excel does not recognize.

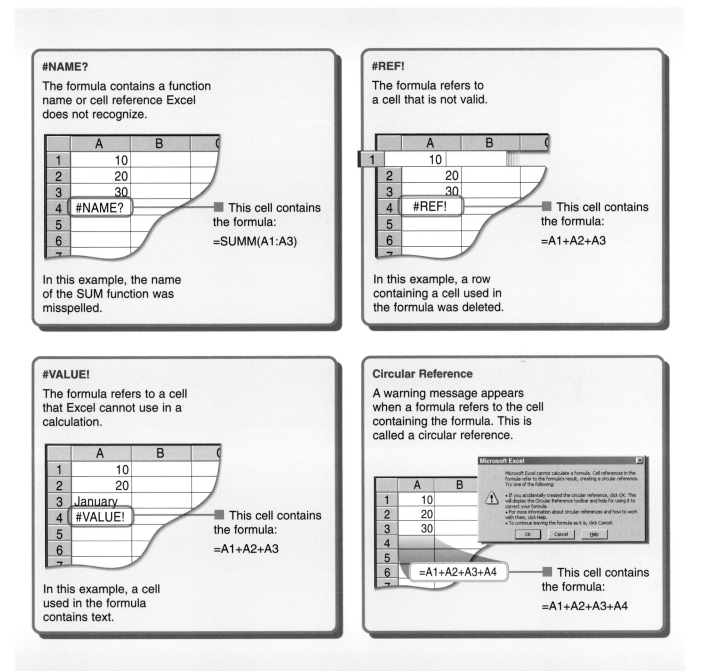

■ This cell contains the formula:

=SUMM(A1:A3)

In this example, the name of the SUM function was misspelled.

#REF!

The formula refers to a cell that is not valid.

■ This cell contains the formula:

=A1+A2+A3

In this example, a row containing a cell used in the formula was deleted.

#VALUE!

The formula refers to a cell that Excel cannot use in a calculation.

■ This cell contains the formula:

=A1+A2+A3

In this example, a cell used in the formula contains text.

Circular Reference

A warning message appears when a formula refers to the cell containing the formula. This is called a circular reference.

Microsoft Excel

Microsoft Excel cannot calculate a formula. Cell references in the formula refer to the formula's result, creating a circular reference. Try one of the following:

• If you accidentally created the circular reference, click OK. This will display the Circular Reference toolbar and help for using it to correct your formula.
• For more information about circular references and how to work with them, click Help.
• To continue leaving the formula as it is, click Cancel.

OK   Cancel   Help

■ This cell contains the formula:

=A1+A2+A3+A4

A scenario is a set of alternate values for data in your worksheet. You can create multiple scenarios to see how different values affect your worksheet data.

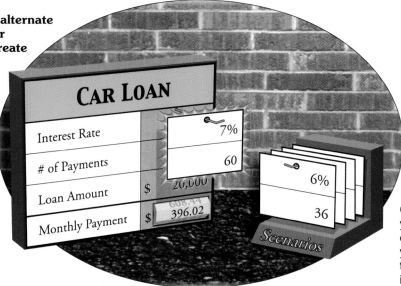

Creating scenarios allows you to consider various outcomes. For example, you can create scenarios to see how changing interest rates will affect your car payments.

CREATE SCENARIOS

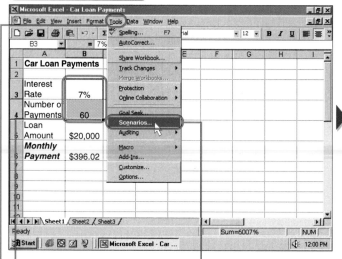

1 Select the cells containing the data you want to change in the scenarios. To select cells, see page 16.

2 Click **Tools**.

3 Click **Scenarios**.

Note: If Scenarios does not appear on the menu, position the mouse ⌖ over the bottom of the menu to display all the menu commands.

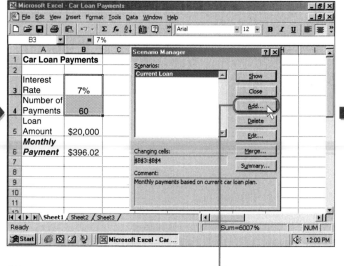

■ The Scenario Manager dialog box appears.

4 Click **Add** to create a new scenario.

Should I save my original data as my first scenario?

Excel will only keep your original data if you save the data as a scenario. After you create a scenario for the original data, you can use the scenario to redisplay the original data at any time.

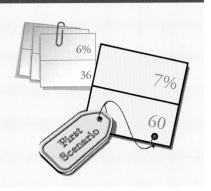

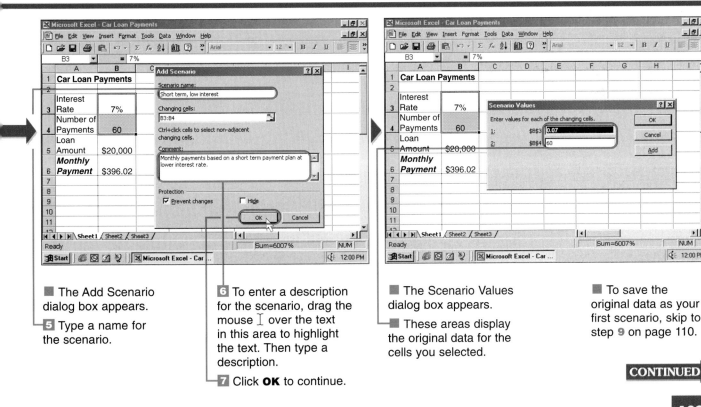

■ The Add Scenario dialog box appears.

5 Type a name for the scenario.

6 To enter a description for the scenario, drag the mouse I over the text in this area to highlight the text. Then type a description.

7 Click **OK** to continue.

■ The Scenario Values dialog box appears.

■ These areas display the original data for the cells you selected.

■ To save the original data as your first scenario, skip to step **9** on page 110.

CONTINUED

CREATE SCENARIOS

Excel saves your scenarios with your worksheet. You can display a different scenario at any time.

CAR LOAN			
Interest Rate	7%		
# of Payments	60		
Loan Amount	$ 20,000		
Monthly Payment	$ 396.02		

6%

36

CREATE SCENARIOS (CONTINUED)

8 To change the values for the scenario, double-click a value and then type a new value. Repeat this step for all the values you want to change.

9 Click **OK** to confirm the values.

■ The Scenario Manager dialog box reappears.

■ The name of the scenario appears in this area.

10 To create another scenario, repeat steps **4** to **9** starting on page 108.

11 When you finish creating scenarios, click **Close** to close the dialog box.

110

How can I move the Scenario Manager dialog box so it is not covering the data in my worksheet?

To move the dialog box, position the mouse ⟍ over the title bar and then drag the dialog box to a new location.

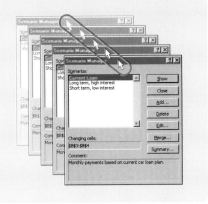

DISPLAY A SCENARIO

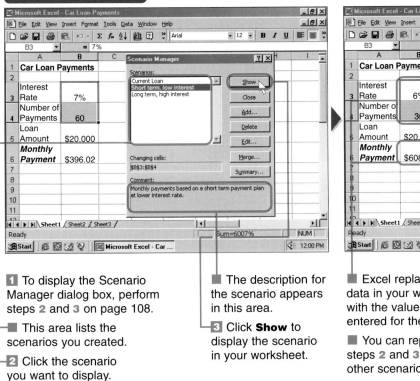

■ To display the Scenario Manager dialog box, perform steps **2** and **3** on page 108.

■ This area lists the scenarios you created.

2 Click the scenario you want to display.

■ The description for the scenario appears in this area.

3 Click **Show** to display the scenario in your worksheet.

■ Excel replaces the data in your worksheet with the values you entered for the scenario.

■ You can repeat steps **2** and **3** to display other scenarios.

4 When you finish displaying scenarios, click **Close** to close the dialog box.

■ The data from the last scenario you displayed remains in your worksheet.

CREATE A SCENARIO SUMMARY REPORT

You can create a summary report to display the values for each scenario and the effects of the scenarios on the calculations in your worksheet.

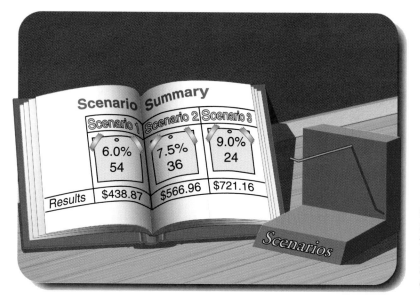

Summary reports are useful when you want to quickly review or print the results of all the scenarios you created.

CREATE A SCENARIO SUMMARY REPORT

1 Click **Tools**.

2 Click **Scenarios**.

Note: If Scenarios does not appear on the menu, position the mouse over the bottom of the menu to display all the menu commands.

■ The Scenario Manager dialog box appears.

3 Click **Summary** to create a summary report.

■ The Scenario Summary dialog box appears.

?

Why does the Scenario Summary worksheet display plus (⊞) and minus (⊟) sign buttons?

Excel groups data together in the Scenario Summary worksheet to make the data easier to work with. You can use the plus and minus sign buttons to hide or display details in each group of data.

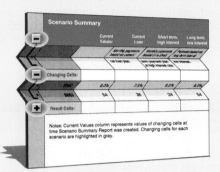

■ Click a plus sign (⊞) to display hidden data.

■ Click a minus sign (⊟) to hide data.

■ This area displays the cell references for each cell Excel will recalculate in the worksheet.

Note: If the correct cell references are not displayed, type each cell reference, separated by a comma (,).

4 Click **Scenario summary** (○ changes to ◉).

5 Click **OK** to create the summary report.

■ Excel creates a worksheet named Scenario Summary to display the summary report.

■ To redisplay the contents of the original worksheet, click the tab of the original worksheet.

Note: For information on working with multiple worksheets, see pages 194 to 203.

Central Division Standings

Pool A	Games	Goals	Wins	Losses	
Walt's Winners	6	15	4	1	
The Chargers	6	13	3	2	
Terry's Tigers	6	12	3	3	
The Breakaways	6	10	1	3	
The GO Team	6	9	1	4	
Pool B	Games		Wins	Losses	
Brian's Boys			4	1	
The Good Guys				1	
Greg 'n' Gang	6	15		2	
The Professionals				3	
All The Way	6	13		3	
Team Spirit	6	1	1	5	

CHAPTER 5

Change Your Screen Display

Are you interested in changing the way your worksheet appears on your screen? In this chapter you will learn how to zoom in and out, hide columns and more.

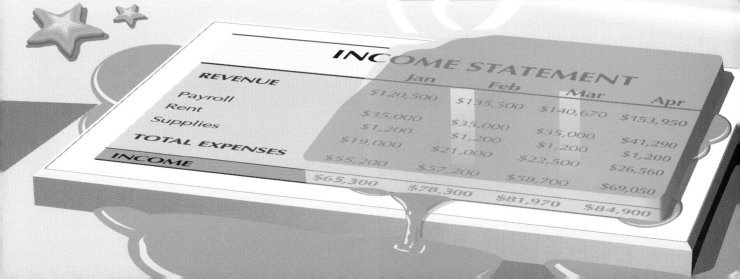

ZOOM IN OR OUT

Excel allows you to enlarge or reduce the display of data on your screen.

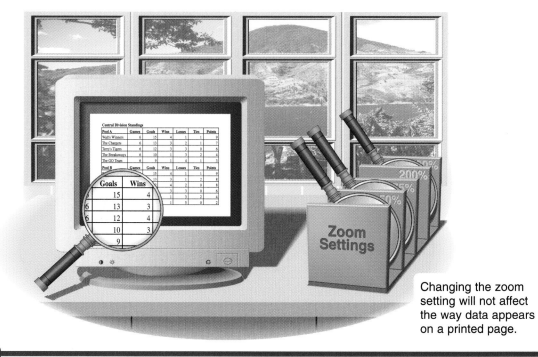

Changing the zoom setting will not affect the way data appears on a printed page.

ZOOM IN OR OUT

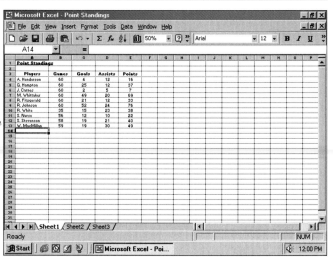

1 Click ▾ in this area to display a list of zoom settings.

Note: If the Zoom area is not displayed, click ░ on the Standard toolbar to display all the buttons.

2 Click the zoom setting you want to use.

■ The worksheet appears in the new zoom setting. You can edit the worksheet as usual.

■ To return to the normal zoom setting, repeat steps **1** and **2**, except select **100%** in step **2**.

You can display a
larger working area
by hiding parts of
the Excel screen.

Using the full screen to
view a worksheet is useful
if you want to display as
many cells as possible
while you review and edit
a large worksheet.

DISPLAY FULL SCREEN

■1 Click **View**.

■2 Click **Full Screen**.

*Note: If Full Screen does not
appear on the menu, position
the mouse ⌖ over the bottom
of the menu to display all the
menu commands.*

■ Excel hides parts of
the screen to display a
larger working area.

■ To once again display
the hidden parts of the
screen, click **Close Full
Screen**.

*Note: You can also repeat
steps 1 and 2 to once again
display the hidden parts of
the screen.*

DISPLAY OR HIDE A TOOLBAR

Excel offers several toolbars that you can display or hide at any time. Each toolbar contains buttons that help you quickly perform common tasks.

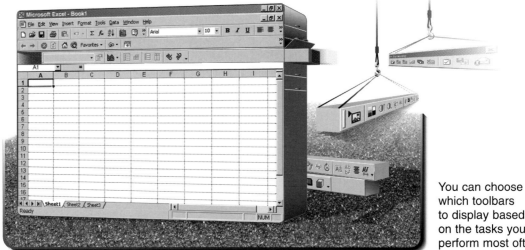

You can choose which toolbars to display based on the tasks you perform most often.

DISPLAY OR HIDE A TOOLBAR

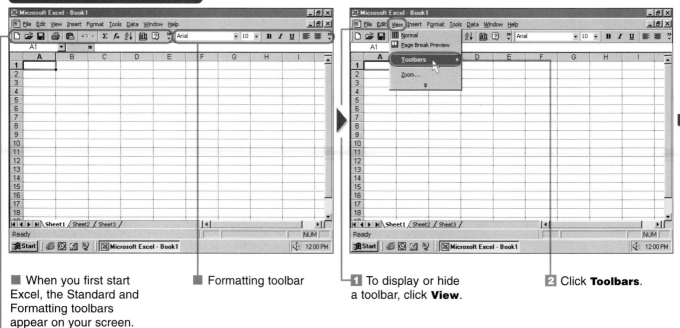

■ When you first start Excel, the Standard and Formatting toolbars appear on your screen.

■ Standard toolbar

■ Formatting toolbar

1 To display or hide a toolbar, click **View**.

2 Click **Toolbars**.

Why would I want to hide a toolbar?

A screen displaying fewer toolbars provides a larger and less cluttered working area.

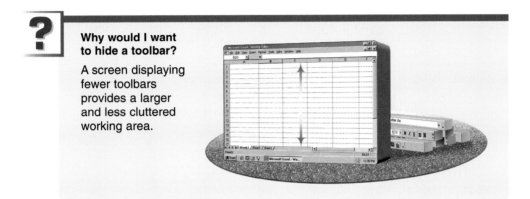

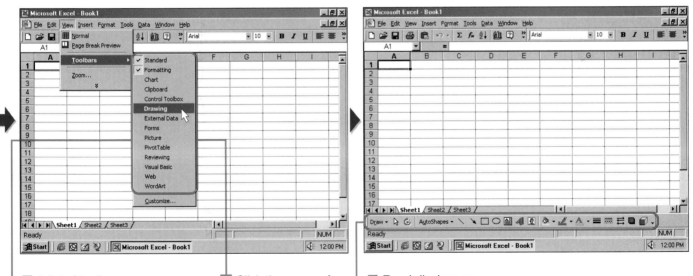

■ A list of toolbars appears. A check mark (✔) beside a toolbar name tells you the toolbar is currently displayed.

3 Click the name of the toolbar you want to display or hide.

■ Excel displays or hides the toolbar you selected.

SIZE A TOOLBAR

You can increase
the size of a
toolbar to display
more buttons on
the toolbar. This
is useful when a
toolbar appears
on the same row
as another toolbar
and cannot display
all of its buttons.

You cannot size
a toolbar that
appears on its
own row.

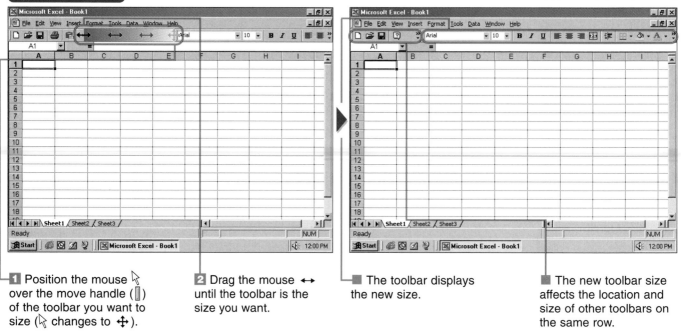

1 Position the mouse
over the move handle (▯)
of the toolbar you want to
size (↳ changes to ✛).

2 Drag the mouse ↔
until the toolbar is the
size you want.

■ The toolbar displays
the new size.

■ The new toolbar size
affects the location and
size of other toolbars on
the same row.

You can move a toolbar to the top, bottom, right or left edge of your screen.

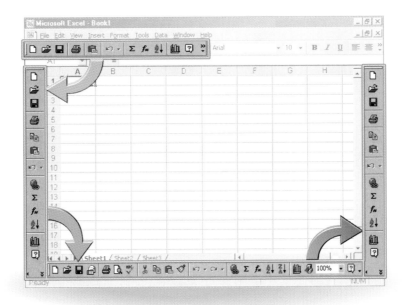

Moving a toolbar to its own row allows you to display more buttons on the toolbar.

MOVE A TOOLBAR

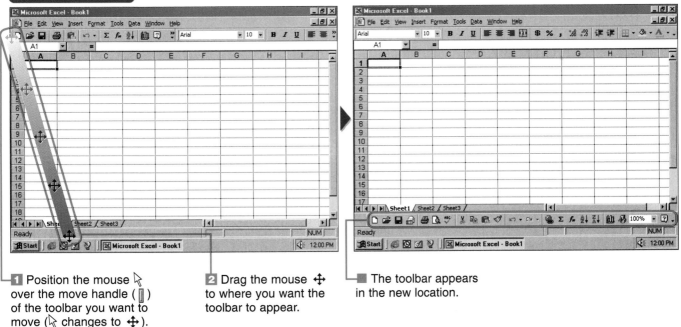

1 Position the mouse ▷ over the move handle (▯) of the toolbar you want to move (▷ changes to ✛).

2 Drag the mouse ✛ to where you want the toolbar to appear.

■ The toolbar appears in the new location.

You can hide rows in your worksheet to temporarily remove unnecessary or confidential data from your screen.

You can hide a single row or multiple rows in your worksheet.

HIDE ROWS

1 Select the rows you want to hide. To select rows, see page 17.

2 Click **Format**.

3 Click **Row**.

4 Click **Hide** to hide the rows.

■ The rows you selected disappear from your worksheet.

?

Will hiding rows affect the formulas and functions in my worksheet?

Hiding rows will not affect the results of formulas and functions in your worksheet. Excel will use data in the hidden rows to perform calculations even though the data is hidden from view. For information on formulas and functions, see pages 86 and 90.

DISPLAY HIDDEN ROWS

1 Select the rows on each side of the hidden rows. To select rows, see page 17.

2 Click **Format**.

3 Click **Row**.

4 Click **Unhide** to display the hidden rows.

■ The hidden rows reappear in your worksheet.

■ To deselect cells, click any cell.

HIDE COLUMNS

You can hide columns in your worksheet to reduce the amount of data displayed on your screen or hide confidential data.

Name	Address	City	State	Zip Code	Pho
Sue Jones	65 Apple Tree Lane	Austin	TX	78710	512-55
Matt Andrews	4 Steven Drive	Miami	FL	33101	305-55
Jim Smith	8910 Colt Rd.	Los Angeles	CA	90011	213-55
Karen Taylor	21 Kirk Drive	Philadelphia	PA	19104	215-55
Mandy Roberts	44 Sunset St.	Little Rock	AR	72231	501-555-
Sam Hunter	689 Walker Ave.	New York	NY	10199	212-555-6
Phillip Morgan	779 Pine St.	Portland	OR	97208	503-555-498

You can hide a single column or multiple columns in your worksheet.

HIDE COLUMNS

1 Select the columns you want to hide. To select columns, see page 17.

2 Click **Format**.

3 Click **Column**.

4 Click **Hide** to hide the columns.

■ The columns you selected disappear from your worksheet.

Do hidden columns appear on a printed page?

Hidden columns will not appear when you print your worksheet. This is useful when you do not want to print columns that contain unneeded or confidential data.

DISPLAY HIDDEN COLUMNS

1 Select the columns on each side of the hidden columns. To select columns, see page 17.

2 Click **Format**.

3 Click **Column**.

4 Click **Unhide** to display the hidden columns.

■ The hidden columns reappear in your worksheet.

■ To deselect cells, click any cell.

FREEZE ROWS AND COLUMNS

You can freeze rows and columns in your worksheet so they will not move. This allows you to keep row and column labels displayed on your screen as you move through a large worksheet.

FREEZE ROWS AND COLUMNS

Excel will freeze the rows above and the columns to the left of the cell you select.

1 To select a cell, click the cell.

2 Click **Window**.

3 Click **Freeze Panes**.

How do I unfreeze rows and columns in my worksheet?

When you no longer want to keep rows and columns frozen on your screen, perform steps **2** and **3** below, except select **Unfreeze Panes** in step **3**.

■ A horizontal line appears in your worksheet.

■ The rows above the horizontal line are frozen. These rows remain on your screen as you move through your worksheet.

■ To move through the rows below the horizontal line, click ▲ or ▼.

■ A vertical line appears in your worksheet.

■ The columns to the left of the vertical line are frozen. These columns remain on your screen as you move through your worksheet.

■ To move through the columns to the right of the vertical line, click ◀ or ▶.

SPLIT A WORKSHEET

You can split your worksheet into separate sections. This allows you to display different areas of a large worksheet at the same time.

SPLIT A WORKSHEET VERTICALLY

1 Position the mouse ⬚ over this area (⬚ changes to ◀╫▶).

2 Drag the mouse ◀╫▶ to where you want to split the worksheet.

■ The worksheet splits vertically into two sections.

■ To move through the columns to the left of the dividing line, click ◀ or ▶.

■ To move through the columns to the right of the dividing line, click ◀ or ▶.

128

?

How do I remove a split from my worksheet?

Position the mouse ⤡ over the dividing line in your worksheet (⤡ changes to ←‖→ or ÷). Then double-click the dividing line to remove the split.

SPLIT A WORKSHEET HORIZONTALLY

	A	B	C	D	E	F	G
1	**Soccer Standings**						
2							
3	Pool A	Games Played	Goals Scored	Wins	Losses	Ties	Poin
4	Brian's Boys	6	15	4	1	1	
5	The Good Guys	6	13	3	1	2	
6	Greg 'n' Gang	6	12	4	2	0	
7	The Professionals	6	12	3	3	0	
8	All The Way	6	8	1	3	2	
9	Team Spirit	6	4	1	5	0	
10							
11	Pool B	Games Played	Goals Scored	Wins	Losses	Ties	Poin
12	We Score	6	16	4	2	0	
13	The Firefighters	6	14	3	2	1	
14	Challengers	6	12	3	3	0	
15	Headers	6	9	2	2	2	
16	The Hurricanes	6	7	1	5	0	

Microsoft Excel - Soccer Standings
File Edit View Insert Format Tools Data Window Help
A18
Ready   NUM
Start   Microsoft Excel - Soc...   12:00 PM

	A	B	C	D	E	F	G
1	**Soccer Standings**						
2							
3	Pool A	Games Played	Goals Scored	Wins	Losses	Ties	Poi
4	Brian's Boys	6	15	4	1	1	
5	The Good Guys	6	13	3	1	2	
6	Greg 'n' Gang	6	12	4	2	0	
7	The Professionals	6	12	3	3	0	
8	All The Way	6	8	1	3	2	
9	Team Spirit	6	4	1	5	0	
10							
11	Pool B	Games Played	Goals Scored	Wins	Losses	Ties	Poi
12	We Score	6	16	4	2	0	
13	The Firefighters	6	14	3	2	1	
14	Challengers	6	12	3	3	0	
15	Headers	6	9	2	2	2	

Microsoft Excel - Soccer Standings
File Edit View Insert Format Tools Data Window Help
A18
Ready   NUM
Start   Microsoft Excel - Soc...   12:00 PM

1 Position the mouse ⤡ over this area (⤡ changes to ÷).

2 Drag the mouse ÷ to where you want to split the worksheet.

■ The worksheet splits horizontally into two sections.

■ To move through the rows above the dividing line, click ▲ or ▼.

■ To move through the rows below the dividing line, click ▲ or ▼.

	Jan	Feb	Mar	Total
East	7	7	5	19
West	6	4	7	17
South	8	7	9	24
Total	21	18	21	60

	Jan	Feb	Mar	Total
East	7	7	5	19
West	6	4	7	17
South	8	7	9	24
Total	21	18	21	60

	Jan	Feb	Mar
East	$ 7	$ 7	$ 5
West	6	4	7
South	8	7	9
Total	$21	$18	$21

Bold *Italic* <u>Underline</u>

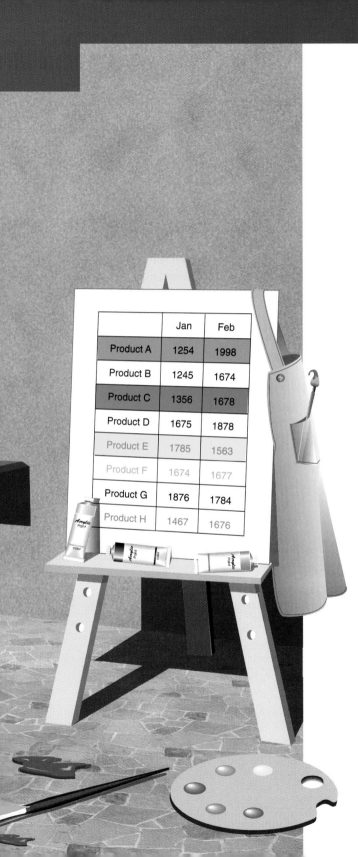

CHAPTER 6

Format Your Worksheets

Would you like to improve the appearance of your worksheet? This chapter shows you how to change the color of data, add borders to cells and much more.

BOLD, ITALICIZE OR UNDERLINE DATA

You can use the Bold, Italic and Underline features to emphasize data in your worksheet.

BOLD, ITALICIZE OR UNDERLINE DATA

1 Select the cells containing the data you want to change. To select cells, see page 16.

2 Click one of these buttons.

B Bold

I Italic

U Underline

Note: If the button you want is not displayed, click ⏵ on the Formatting toolbar to display all the buttons.

■ The data appears in the new style.

■ To deselect cells, click any cell.

■ To remove a bold, italic or underline style, repeat steps 1 and 2.

CHANGE HORIZONTAL ALIGNMENT OF DATA

You can change the
way Excel positions
data between the
left and right edges
of a cell in your
worksheet.

Excel automatically
left aligns text and
right aligns numbers
and dates you enter
into cells.

CHANGE HORIZONTAL ALIGNMENT OF DATA

1 Select the cells
containing the data you
want to align differently. To
select cells, see page 16.

2 Click one of these
buttons.

📄 Left align

📄 Center

📄 Right align

*Note: If the button you want
is not displayed, click* 📄
*on the Formatting toolbar
to display all the buttons.*

■ Excel aligns the data.

■ To deselect cells,
click any cell.

CHANGE FONT OF DATA

You can enhance the appearance of your worksheet by changing the design, or font, of data.

CHANGE FONT OF DATA

1 Select the cells containing the data you want to change. To select cells, see page 16.

2 Click ☐ in this area to display a list of the available fonts.

Note: If the Font area is not displayed, click ☒ on the Formatting toolbar to display all the buttons.

3 Click the font you want to use.

■ The data changes to the font you selected.

■ To deselect cells, click any cell.

134

CHANGE SIZE OF DATA

You can increase
or decrease the
size of data in
your worksheet.

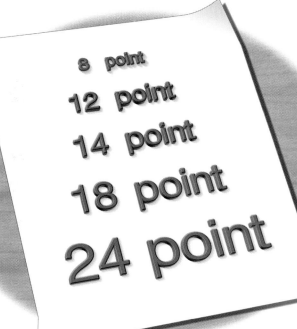

8 point

12 point

14 point

18 point

24 point

Excel measures the
size of data in points.
There are 72 points
in one inch.

CHANGE SIZE OF DATA

1 Select the cells
containing the data you
want to change. To select
cells, see page 16.

2 Click ☐ in this area
to display a list of the
available sizes.

*Note: If the Font Size area is
not displayed, click ☐ on the
Formatting toolbar to display
all the buttons.*

3 Click the size you
want to use.

■ The data changes to
the size you selected.

■ To deselect cells,
click any cell.

CHANGE FONT FOR ALL NEW WORKBOOKS

You can change the font that Excel uses for all new workbooks you create. This is useful when you want all future workbooks to appear in a specific font.

CHANGE FONT FOR ALL NEW WORKBOOKS

1 Click **Tools**.

2 Click **Options**.

■ The Options dialog box appears.

3 Click the **General** tab.

4 To select the font you want to use for all your new workbooks, click ▾ in this area.

5 Click the font you want to use.

Will changing the font for all new workbooks affect the workbooks I have already created?

No. Excel will not change the font in workbooks you have already created. To change the font of data in existing workbooks, see pages 134 and 135.

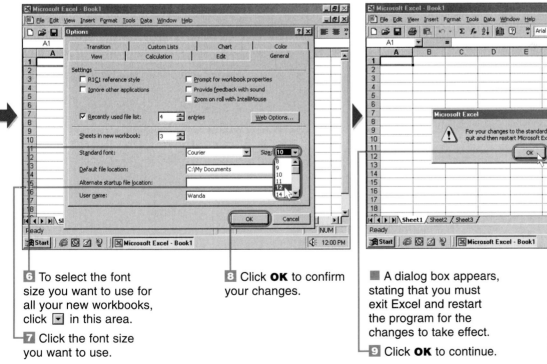

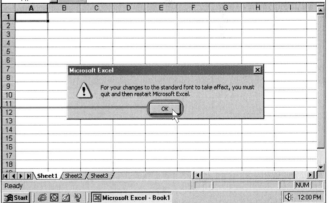

■ **6** To select the font size you want to use for all your new workbooks, click ▼ in this area.

■ **7** Click the font size you want to use.

■ **8** Click **OK** to confirm your changes.

■ A dialog box appears, stating that you must exit Excel and restart the program for the changes to take effect.

■ **9** Click **OK** to continue.

■ You must now exit and restart Excel to use the font in new workbooks you create. To exit Excel, see page 37. To restart Excel, see page 7.

CHANGE APPEARANCE OF DATA

You can make data in your worksheet look more attractive by using various fonts, styles, sizes, underlines, colors and special effects.

ABC Company Soccer Tournament

	Wins	Losses	Ties	Points
Brian's Boys	4	2	1	9
Team Spirit	3	2	1	7
We Score	2	1	2	6
Headers	1	4	2	3
The Good Guys	3	1	0	8
Greg 'n' Gang	4	3	2	8
Challengers	2	1		5
	3			8

Fonts
Styles
Sizes
Underlines
Colors
Special Effects

CHANGE APPEARANCE OF DATA

1 Select the cells containing the data you want to change. To select cells, see page 16.

2 Click **Format**.

3 Click **Cells**.

■ The Format Cells dialog box appears.

? **What determines which fonts are available in Excel?**

The available fonts depend on the fonts installed on your computer and printer. Excel includes several fonts, but additional fonts may be available from the other programs on your computer. Your printer may also have built-in fonts you can use.

4 Click the **Font** tab.

5 To select a font for the data, click the font you want to use.

6 To select a style for the data, click the style you want to use.

7 To select a size for the data, click the size you want to use.

■ This area displays a preview of how the data will appear in your worksheet.

CONTINUED

CHANGE APPEARANCE OF DATA

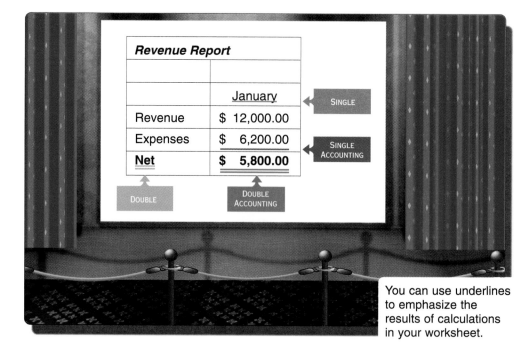

Excel offers several underline styles you can use to underline data in your worksheet.

You can use underlines to emphasize the results of calculations in your worksheet.

CHANGE APPEARANCE OF DATA (CONTINUED)

8 To select an underline style for the data, click this area.

9 Click the underline style you want to use.

10 To select a color for the data, click this area.

11 Click the color you want to use.

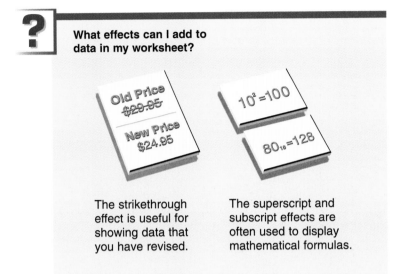

What effects can I add to data in my worksheet?

The strikethrough effect is useful for showing data that you have revised.

The superscript and subscript effects are often used to display mathematical formulas.

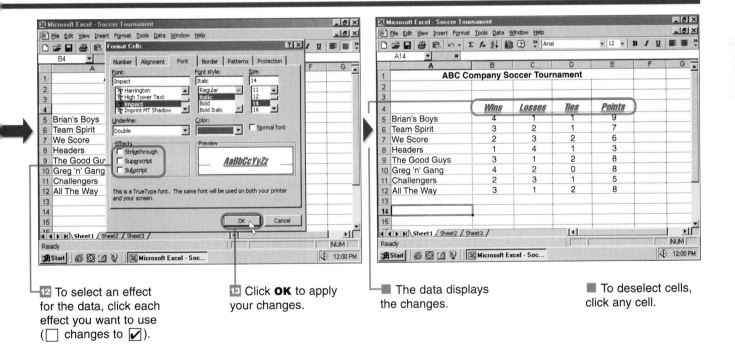

12 To select an effect for the data, click each effect you want to use (☐ changes to ☑).

13 Click **OK** to apply your changes.

■ The data displays the changes.

■ To deselect cells, click any cell.

CHANGE CELL OR DATA COLOR

You can make your worksheet more attractive by adding color to cells or data.

CHANGE CELL COLOR

1 Select the cells you want to change to a different color. To select cells, see page 16.

2 Click ▾ in this area to select a color.

Note: If ▨▾ is not displayed, click ▨ on the Formatting toolbar to display all the buttons.

3 Click the color you want to use.

■ The cells display the new color.

■ To deselect cells, click any cell.

■ To remove a color from cells, repeat steps **1** to **3**, except select **No Fill** in step **3**.

?

What colors should I choose?

When adding color to your worksheet, make sure you choose cell and data colors that work well together. For example, red data on a blue background is difficult to read.

CHANGE DATA COLOR

1 Select the cells containing the data you want to change to a different color. To select cells, see page 16.

2 Click ⬝ in this area to select a color.

Note: If ⬝A⬝ is not displayed, click ⬝ on the Formatting toolbar to display all the buttons.

3 Click the color you want to use.

■ The data displays the new color.

■ To deselect cells, click any cell.

■ To remove a color from data, repeat steps **1** to **3**, except select **Automatic** in step **3**.

INDENT DATA

You can indent data to move the data away from the left edge of a cell.

1 Select the cells containing the data you want to indent. To select cells, see page 16.

2 Click ⬛ to indent the data.

Note: If ⬛ is not displayed, click ❯ on the Formatting toolbar to display all the buttons.

◼ Excel indents the data.

◼ To deselect cells, click any cell.

◼ To remove the indent, repeat steps **1** and **2**, except click ⬛ in step **2**.

Note: If ⬛ is not displayed, click ❯ on the Formatting toolbar to display all the buttons.

You can center data
across several columns
in your worksheet. This
is useful for centering
titles over your data.

CENTER DATA ACROSS COLUMNS

1 Select the cells you
want to center the data
across. To select cells,
see page 16.

*Note: The first cell you select
should contain the data you
want to center.*

2 Click 🔲 to center
the data.

*Note: If 🔲 is not displayed,
click 》 on the Formatting
toolbar to display all the
buttons.*

■ Excel centers the
data across the cells
you selected.

WRAP TEXT IN CELLS

You can display
long lines of text
within cells by
wrapping the text.

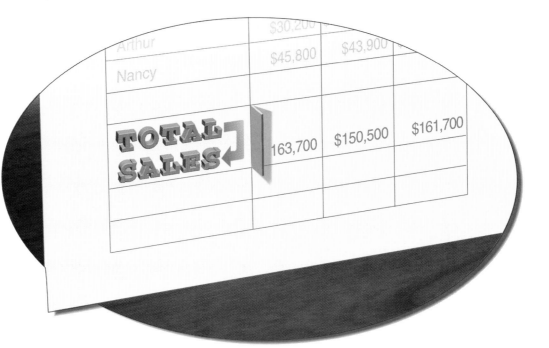

WRAP TEXT IN CELLS

1 Select the cells
containing the text you
want to wrap. To select
cells, see page 16.

2 Click **Format**.

3 Click **Cells**.

■ The Format Cells
dialog box appears.

Can I display all the text in a cell without wrapping the text?

You can have Excel reduce the size of text to fit within a cell. Perform steps 1 to 6 below, except select **Shrink to fit** in step 5 (☐ changes to ☑).

If you later change the width of the column, Excel will automatically adjust the size of the text to fit the new width.

4 Click the **Alignment** tab.

5 Click **Wrap text** (☐ changes to ☑).

6 Click **OK** to confirm your change.

■ The text wraps within the cells you selected. The row heights change to fit the wrapped text.

■ To deselect cells, click any cell.

CHANGE VERTICAL ALIGNMENT OF DATA

You can change the
way Excel positions
data between the top
and bottom edges of a
cell in your worksheet.

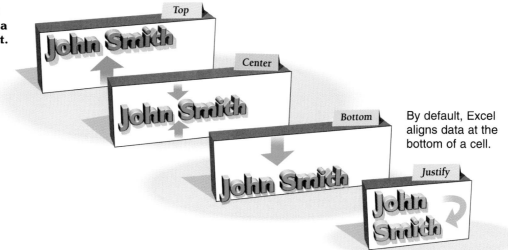

Top

Center

Bottom

By default, Excel
aligns data at the
bottom of a cell.

Justify

CHANGE VERTICAL ALIGNMENT OF DATA

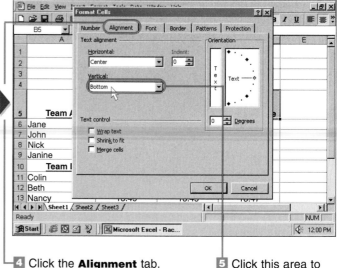

1 Select the cells
containing the data you
want to align differently.
To select cells, see
page 16.

2 Click **Format**.

3 Click **Cells**.

■ The Format Cells
dialog box appears.

4 Click the **Alignment** tab.

5 Click this area to
select the way you
want to align the data.

? **Why didn't I see a change when I vertically aligned my data?**

You may need to increase the height of the row to view the data in the new alignment. To change the height of rows, see page 69.

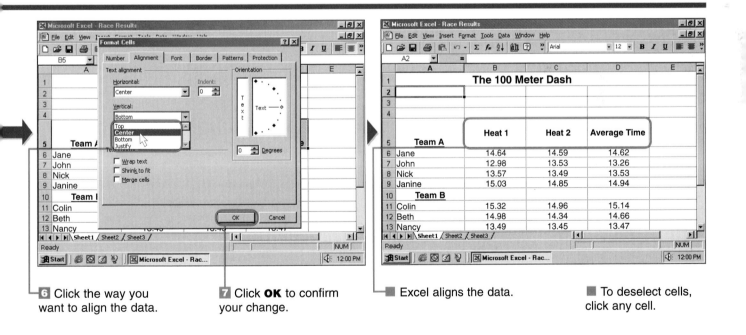

6 Click the way you want to align the data.

7 Click **OK** to confirm your change.

■ Excel aligns the data.

■ To deselect cells, click any cell.

You can rotate data within cells in your worksheet. This is useful for emphasizing row and column labels.

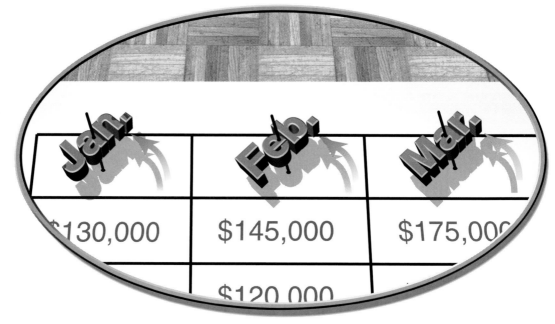

ROTATE DATA IN CELLS

1 Select the cells containing the data you want to rotate. To select cells, see page 16.

2 Click **Format**.

3 Click **Cells**.

■ The Format Cells dialog box appears.

4 Click the **Alignment** tab.

■ This area displays the way your data will appear in the selected cells.

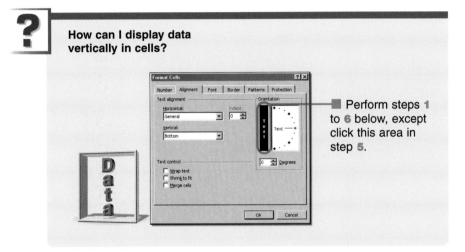

How can I display data vertically in cells?

■ Perform steps 1 to 6 below, except click this area in step 5.

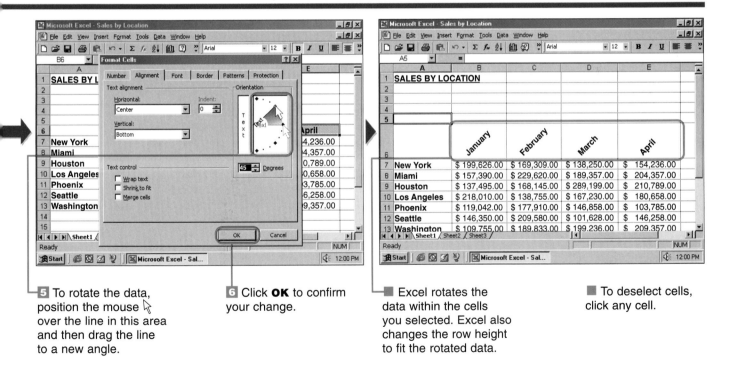

■ **5** To rotate the data, position the mouse over the line in this area and then drag the line to a new angle.

■ **6** Click **OK** to confirm your change.

■ Excel rotates the data within the cells you selected. Excel also changes the row height to fit the rotated data.

■ To deselect cells, click any cell.

COPY FORMATTING

Once you format one cell to suit your needs, you can make other cells look exactly the same.

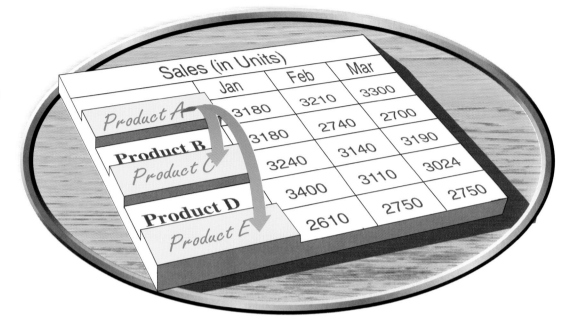

1 Click a cell displaying the formatting you want to copy.

2 Click ✎ to copy the formatting.

Note: If ✎ is not displayed, click ⚹ on the Standard toolbar to display all the buttons.

■ The mouse ⇩ changes to ⇩▪ when over your worksheet.

3 Select the cells you want to display the formatting. To select cells, see page 16.

What types of formatting can I copy?

You can copy a combination of number, data and cell formatting.

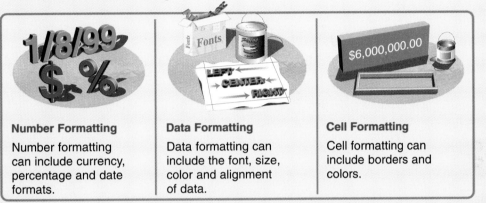

Number Formatting

Number formatting can include currency, percentage and date formats.

Data Formatting

Data formatting can include the font, size, color and alignment of data.

Cell Formatting

Cell formatting can include borders and colors.

■ The cells display the formatting.

■ To deselect cells, click any cell.

COPY FORMATTING TO SEVERAL AREAS

1 Click a cell displaying the formatting you want to copy.

2 Double-click ✎ to copy the formatting.

Note: If ✎ is not displayed, click ▸ on the Standard toolbar to display all the buttons.

3 Select each group of cells you want to display the formatting.

4 When you finish copying the formatting, press the Esc key.

ADD BORDERS

You can add borders to enhance the appearance of your worksheet. You can also use borders to divide your worksheet into sections.

	Jan	Feb
Product A	1254	1998
Product B	1245	1674
Product C	1356	1678
Product D	1675	1878
Product E	1785	1563
Product F	1674	1677
Product G	1876	1784
Product H	1467	1676

ADD BORDERS

■ Select the cells you want to display borders. To select cells, see page 16.

■2 Click ⊡ in this area to display the types of borders you can add to the cells.

Note: If ⊞⊡ is not displayed, click ⊠ on the Formatting toolbar to display all the buttons.

■3 Click the type of border you want to add.

■ The cells display the border you selected.

■ To deselect cells, click any cell.

■ To remove the borders from cells, repeat steps 1 to 3, except select ⊞ in step 3.

154

You can remove
all the formatting
from cells in your
worksheet.

CLEAR FORMATTING

1 Select the cells
containing the formatting
you want to remove. To
select cells, see page 16.

2 Click **Edit**.

3 Click **Clear**.

4 Click **Formats**.

■ All the formatting
disappears from the
cells you selected.

■ To deselect cells,
click any cell.

*Note: If you clear the formatting
from cells containing dates, the
dates change to numbers. To
once again display the dates,
you must change the format of
the cells to the Date format. For
more information, see page 158.*

CHANGE NUMBER FORMAT

You can change the appearance of numbers in your worksheet without retyping the numbers.

SALES		
Salesperson	Jan	Feb
Richard	1564	1687
Nancy	2008	2114
Steve	1789	1487
Jason	1002	1298
Susan	2354	1809
Dan	3500	2500
Scott	1170	2200
Cathy	2360	1479

SALES		
Salesperson	Jan	Feb
Richard	$1,564.00	$1,687.00
Nancy	$2,008.00	$2,114.00
Steve	$1,789.00	$1,487.00
Jason	$1,002.00	$1,298.00
Susan	$2,354.00	$1,809.00
Dan	$3,500.00	$2,500.00
Scott	$1,170.00	$2,200.00
Cathy	$2,360.00	$1,479.00

When you change the format of numbers, you do not change the value of the numbers.

CHANGE THE NUMBER STYLE

1 Select the cells containing the numbers you want to change. To select cells, see page 16.

2 Click one of these buttons.

- **$** Currency
- **%** Percent
- **,** Comma

Note: If the button you want is not displayed, click [»] on the Formatting toolbar to display all the buttons.

■ The numbers display the style you selected.

■ To deselect cells, click any cell.

How can I format the numbers in my worksheet?

Option		Example
$	Change to dollar value	10 → $10.00
%	Change to percentage	0.15 → 15%
,	Add comma and display two decimal places	1000 → 1,000.00
.00	Add decimal place	10.13 → 10.130
.00	Remove decimal place	10.13 → 10.1

ADD OR REMOVE A DECIMAL PLACE

1 Select the cells containing the numbers you want to change. To select cells, see page 16.

2 Click one of these buttons.

.00 Add decimal place

.00 Remove decimal place

Note: If the button you want is not displayed, click ⊠ on the Formatting toolbar to display all the buttons.

■ Excel increases or decreases the number of decimal places.

■ To deselect cells, click any cell.

CHANGE NUMBER FORMAT

Excel offers many different formats that you can use to make the numbers in your worksheet easier to read.

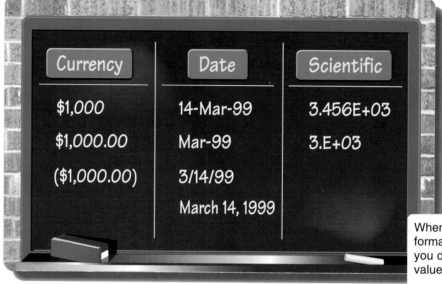

Currency	Date	Scientific
$1,000	14-Mar-99	3.456E+03
$1,000.00	Mar-99	3.E+03
($1,000.00)	3/14/99	
	March 14, 1999	

When you change the format of numbers, you do not change the value of the numbers.

USING THE FORMAT CELLS DIALOG BOX

1 Select the cells containing the numbers you want to change. To select cells, see page 16.

2 Click **Format**.

3 Click **Cells**.

■ The Format Cells dialog box appears.

4 Click the **Number** tab.

5 Click the category that describes the numbers in the cells you selected.

■ This area displays all the options for the category you selected. Each category displays a different set of options.

?

Why did number signs (#) appear in a cell after I changed the number format?

If number signs (#) appear in a cell, the column is not wide enough to display the entire number. To change the column width, see page 68.

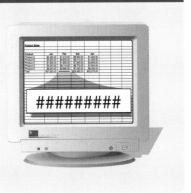

#########

6 To select the number of decimal places you want the numbers to display, double-click this area. Then type the number of decimal places.

7 To select the way you want negative numbers to appear, click one of the available styles.

8 Click **OK** to apply your changes.

■ The numbers display the changes.

■ To deselect cells, click any cell.

APPLY AN AUTOFORMAT

Excel offers many
ready-to-use designs,
called AutoFormats,
that you can choose
from to give your
worksheet a new
appearance.

APPLY AN AUTOFORMAT

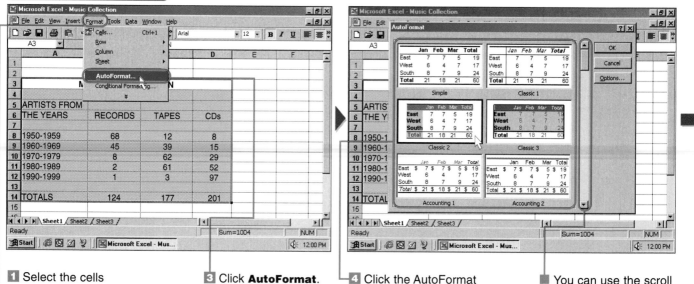

1 Select the cells
you want to apply an
AutoFormat to. To select
cells, see page 16.

2 Click **Format**.

3 Click **AutoFormat**.

■ The AutoFormat
dialog box appears.

4 Click the AutoFormat
you want to use.

■ You can use the scroll
bar to browse through the
available AutoFormats.

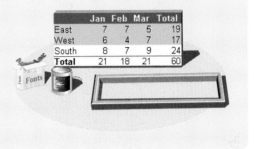

What formatting does an AutoFormat include?

Each AutoFormat includes a combination of formats, such as text and number styles, fonts, colors and borders that you can use to create a professional-looking worksheet.

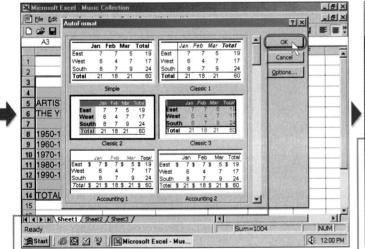

5 Click **OK** to apply the AutoFormat to the cells you selected.

■ The cells display the AutoFormat you selected.

■ To deselect cells, click any cell.

■ To remove an AutoFormat, repeat steps **1** to **5**, except select **None** in step **4**.

APPLY CONDITIONAL FORMATTING

You can have Excel apply formatting to data when the data meets a condition you specify. This can help you quickly locate important data on a large worksheet.

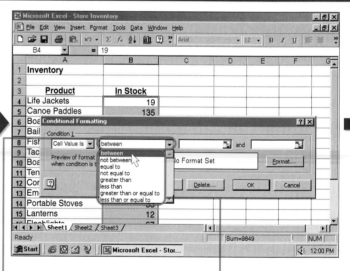

For example, when the number of units in stock falls below 10, you can have Excel display the number in red.

APPLY CONDITIONAL FORMATTING

1 Select the cells containing the data you want Excel to format when the data meets a condition. To select cells, see page 16.

2 Click **Format**.

3 Click **Conditional Formatting**.

■ The Conditional Formatting dialog box appears.

4 Click this area to select an operator for the condition.

5 Click the operator you want to use.

Note: For information on operators, see the top of page 163.

? What is an operator?

An operator tells Excel how to compare the data in a cell to the value you specify. For example, you can use the **greater than** operator when you want Excel to determine whether the data in a cell has a value of more than 100.

greater than **100**

6 Click this area and then type the value you want to use for the condition.

7 If you selected **between** or **not between** in step **5**, click this area and then type the second value.

8 Click **Format** to specify how you want to format the data when the data meets the condition.

■ The Format Cells dialog box appears.

CONTINUED

APPLY CONDITIONAL FORMATTING

You can specify
the color and font
style you want to
use for data that
meets a condition.

9 To select a color for the data, click this area.

10 Click the color you want to use.

11 To select a font style for the data, click the font style you want to use.

■ This area displays a preview of the options you selected.

12 Click **OK** to confirm your changes.

Can I copy conditional formatting?

Yes. Copying conditional formatting is useful when you want other cells in your worksheet to display the same formatting under the same conditions. You can copy conditional formatting as you would copy any formatting in your worksheet. To copy formatting, see page 152.

■ This area displays how data that meets the condition will appear in your worksheet.

13 Click **OK** to confirm your changes.

■ The data in the cells you selected displays the formatting if the data meets the condition you specified.

■ To deselect cells, click any cell.

REMOVE CONDITIONAL FORMATTING

1 To remove conditional formatting from cells, perform steps 1 to 4 on page 155 to clear the formatting.

CHAPTER 7

Print Your Worksheets

Are you ready to print your worksheet? In this chapter you will learn how to preview your worksheet and change the way your worksheet appears on a printed page.

PREVIEW A WORKSHEET

You can use the
Print Preview feature
to see how your
worksheet will
look when printed.

Previewing a worksheet
lets you confirm the
worksheet will print
the way you want.

PREVIEW A WORKSHEET

1 Click 🔍 to preview
your worksheet.

*Note: If 🔍 is not displayed,
click ⋮ on the Standard toolbar
to display all the buttons.*

■ The Print Preview
window appears.

■ This area indicates
which page is displayed
and the total number of
pages in your worksheet.

2 If your worksheet
contains more than one
page, you can click **Next**
or **Previous** to view the
next or previous page.

■ You can also use
the scroll bar to view
other pages.

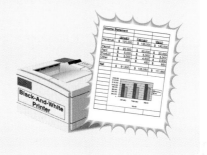

Why does my worksheet appear in black and white in the Print Preview window?

If you are using a black-and-white printer, your worksheet appears in black and white in the Print Preview window. If you are using a color printer, your worksheet appears in color.

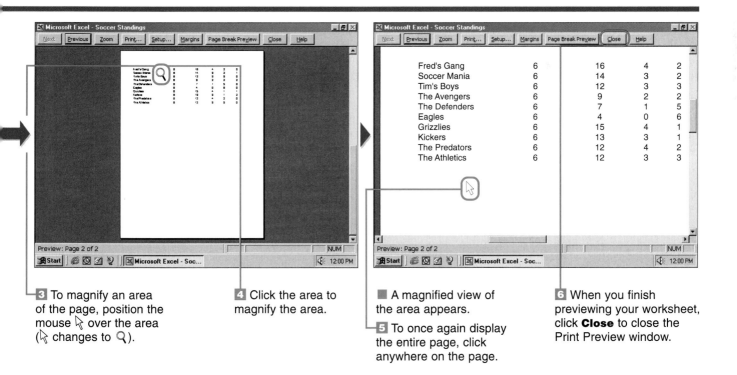

Fred's Gang	6	16	4	2
Soccer Mania	6	14	3	2
Tim's Boys	6	12	3	3
The Avengers	6	9	2	2
The Defenders	6	7	1	5
Eagles	6	4	0	6
Grizzlies	6	15	4	1
Kickers	6	13	3	1
The Predators	6	12	4	2
The Athletics	6	12	3	3

3 To magnify an area of the page, position the mouse over the area (changes to 🔍).

4 Click the area to magnify the area.

■ A magnified view of the area appears.

5 To once again display the entire page, click anywhere on the page.

6 When you finish previewing your worksheet, click **Close** to close the Print Preview window.

PRINT A WORKSHEET

You can produce a paper copy of the worksheet displayed on your screen.

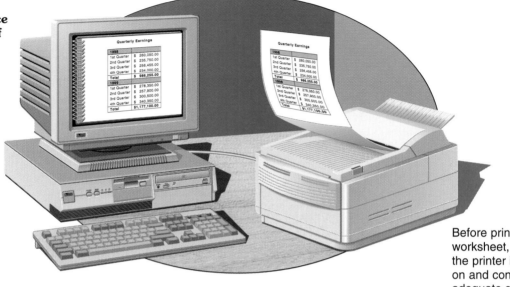

Before printing your worksheet, make sure the printer is turned on and contains an adequate supply of paper.

PRINT A WORKSHEET

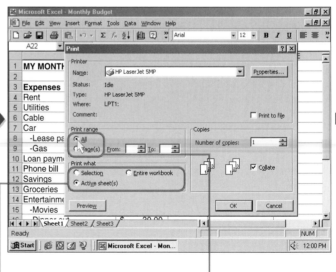

1 Click any cell in the worksheet you want to print.

■ To print only specific cells in the worksheet, select the cells you want to print. To select cells, see page 16.

2 Click **File**.

3 Click **Print**.

■ The Print dialog box appears.

4 Click the part of the workbook you want to print (○ changes to ⊙).

5 If the part of the workbook you selected to print contains more than one page, click an option to specify which pages you want to print (○ changes to ⊙).

? What part of a workbook can I print?

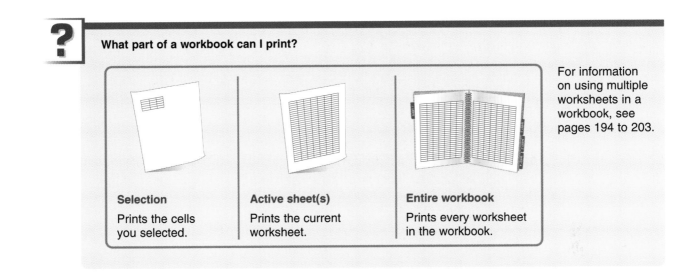

Selection

Prints the cells you selected.

Active sheet(s)

Prints the current worksheet.

Entire workbook

Prints every worksheet in the workbook.

For information on using multiple worksheets in a workbook, see pages 194 to 203.

For information on using multiple worksheets in a workbook, see pages 194 to 203.

■ If you selected **Page(s)** in step **5**, type the number of the first page you want to print. Press the `Tab` key and then type the number of the last page you want to print.

6 Click **OK**.

QUICKLY PRINT ENTIRE WORKSHEET

1 Click 🖨 to quickly print the worksheet displayed on your screen.

Note: If 🖨 is not displayed, click 🔽 on the Standard toolbar to display all the buttons.

SET A PRINT AREA

If you always print
the same area of your
worksheet, you can set
a print area to quickly
print the data. Excel
will print only the data
in the print area.

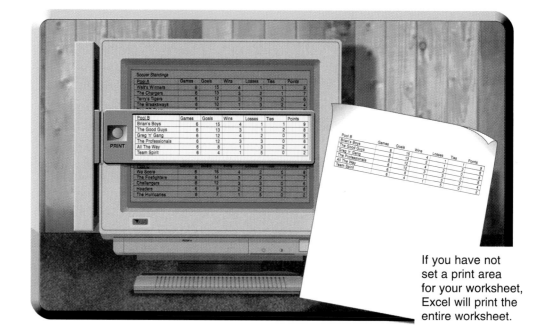

If you have not
set a print area
for your worksheet,
Excel will print the
entire worksheet.

SET A PRINT AREA

1 Select the cells
containing the data you
want to include in the
print area. To select
cells, see page 16.

2 Click **File**.

3 Click **Print Area**.

4 Click **Set Print Area**.

?

How do I print other data in my worksheet after I set a print area?

You can temporarily override a print area you have set and print other data in your worksheet. Select the cells containing the data you want to print and then perform steps **2** to **6** starting on page 170, choosing **Selection** in step **4** (○ changes to ⊙).

CLICK · Override Print Area

■ A dotted line appears around the cells you selected.

■ To deselect cells, click any cell.

PRINT A PRINT AREA

1 Click 🖨 to print the data in the print area at any time.

CLEAR A PRINT AREA

1 Click **File**.

2 Click **Print Area**.

3 Click **Clear Print Area** to clear the print area from your worksheet.

■ The dotted line disappears from your worksheet.

CENTER DATA ON A PAGE

You can center data horizontally and vertically between the margins on a page.

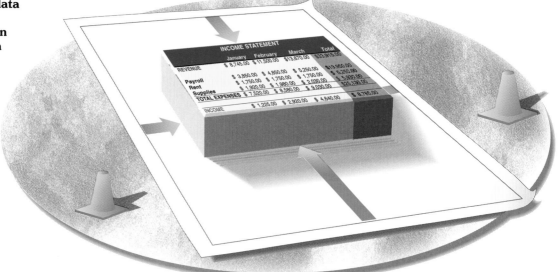

CENTER DATA ON A PAGE

1 Click **File**.

2 Click **Page Setup**.

■ The Page Setup dialog box appears.

3 Click the **Margins** tab.

4 Click the way you want to center the data (☐ changes to ☑). You can select both center options if you wish.

5 Click **OK** to confirm your change.

■ Centering data on a page changes the way your worksheet appears on a printed page, but does not affect the way the worksheet appears on your screen.

You can change
the orientation
of your printed
worksheet.

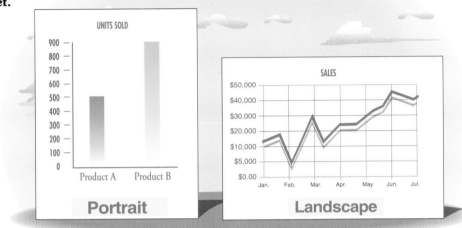

Portrait

Landscape

Excel automatically
prints worksheets in the
portrait orientation. The
landscape orientation is
useful when you want a
wide worksheet to fit on
one printed page.

CHANGE PAGE ORIENTATION

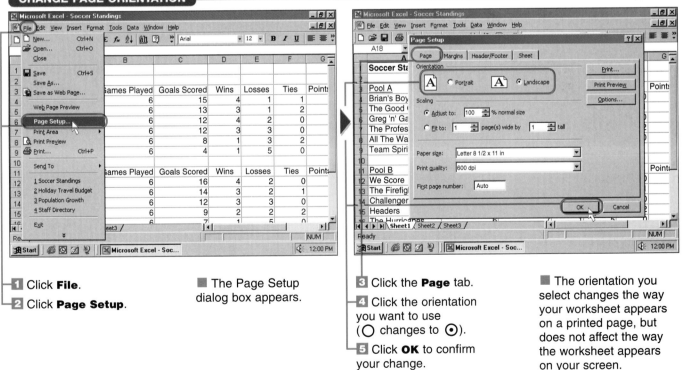

■1 Click **File**.

■2 Click **Page Setup**.

■ The Page Setup
dialog box appears.

■3 Click the **Page** tab.

■4 Click the orientation
you want to use
(○ changes to ⊙).

■5 Click **OK** to confirm
your change.

■ The orientation you
select changes the way
your worksheet appears
on a printed page, but
does not affect the way
the worksheet appears
on your screen.

CHANGE MARGINS

A margin is the amount of space between data and an edge of your paper. You can change the margins for your worksheet.

Excel automatically sets the top and bottom margins to 1 inch and the left and right margins to 0.75 inches.

CHANGE MARGINS

1 Click 🔍 to display your worksheet in the Print Preview window. This window allows you to change the margins.

Note: If 🔍 is not displayed, click 👋 on the Standard toolbar to display all the buttons.

■ The worksheet appears in the Print Preview window.

Note: For information on the Print Preview feature, see page 168.

2 If the margins are not displayed, click **Margins**.

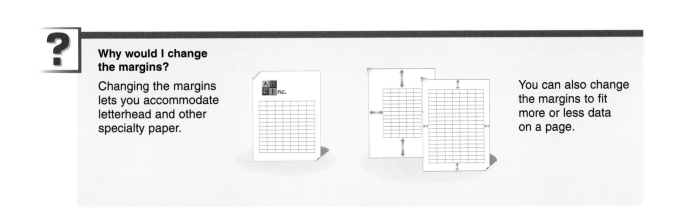

Why would I change the margins?

Changing the margins lets you accommodate letterhead and other specialty paper.

You can also change the margins to fit more or less data on a page.

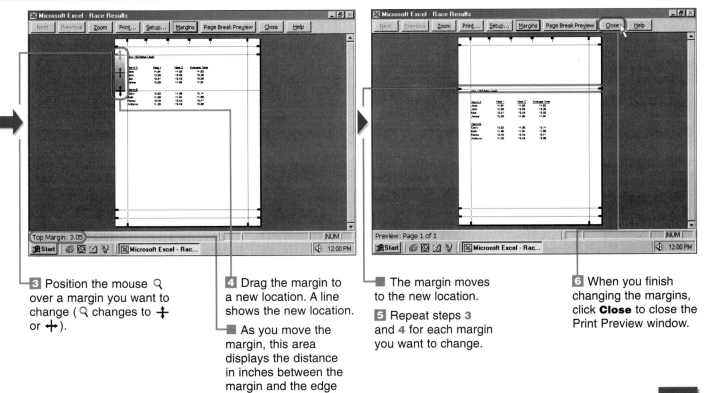

3 Position the mouse ⚲ over a margin you want to change (⚲ changes to ╬ or ↔).

4 Drag the margin to a new location. A line shows the new location.

■ As you move the margin, this area displays the distance in inches between the margin and the edge of the page.

■ The margin moves to the new location.

5 Repeat steps **3** and **4** for each margin you want to change.

6 When you finish changing the margins, click **Close** to close the Print Preview window.

CHANGE PRINT OPTIONS

Excel offers several
print options that let
you change the way
your worksheet appears
on a printed page.

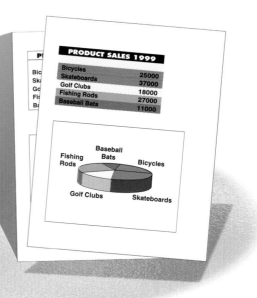

PRODUCT SALES 1999

Bicycles	
Skateboards	25000
Golf Clubs	37000
Fishing Rods	18000
Baseball Bats	27000
	11000

---

1 Click **File**.

2 Click **Page Setup**.

■ The Page Setup
dialog box appears.

3 Click the **Sheet** tab.

4 Click each print
option you want to use
(☐ changes to ☑).

178

What are the print options Excel offers?

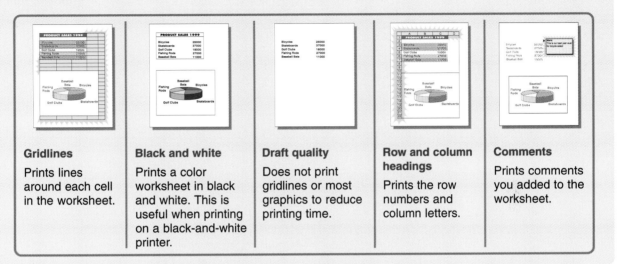

Gridlines

Prints lines around each cell in the worksheet.

Black and white

Prints a color worksheet in black and white. This is useful when printing on a black-and-white printer.

Draft quality

Does not print gridlines or most graphics to reduce printing time.

Row and column headings

Prints the row numbers and column letters.

Comments

Prints comments you added to the worksheet.

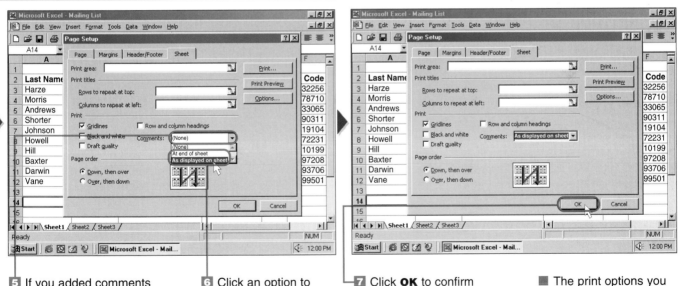

5 If you added comments to the worksheet, click this area to print the comments.

Note: For information on comments, see pages 80 to 83.

6 Click an option to specify where you want to print the comments.

At end of sheet
Print comments on separate page

As displayed on sheet
Print comments on worksheet

7 Click **OK** to confirm your changes.

■ The print options you select change the way your worksheet appears on a printed page, but do not affect the way the worksheet appears on your screen.

INSERT A PAGE BREAK

You can insert a page
break when you want
to start a new page at
a specific place in your
worksheet. A page
break indicates where
one page ends and
another begins.

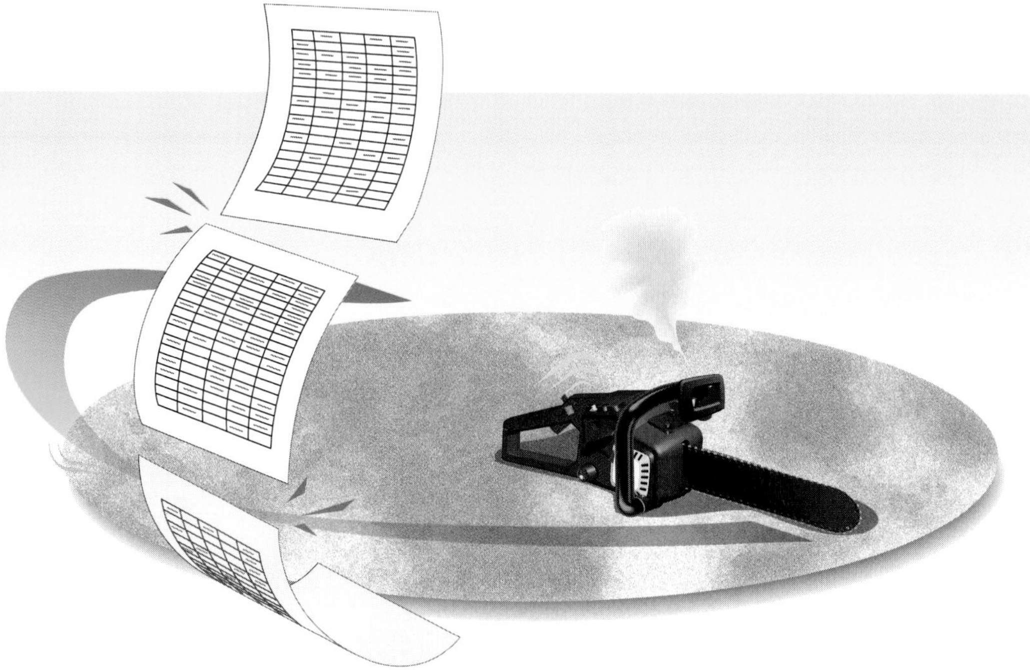

INSERT A PAGE BREAK

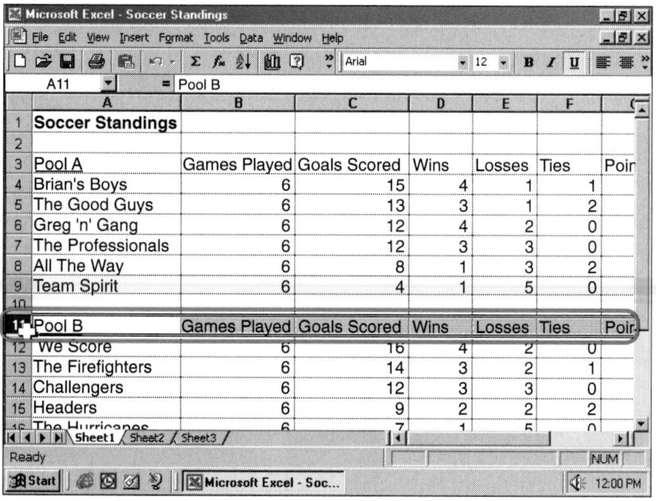

1 To select the row
or column you want to
appear at the beginning
of the new page, click
the heading of the row
or column.

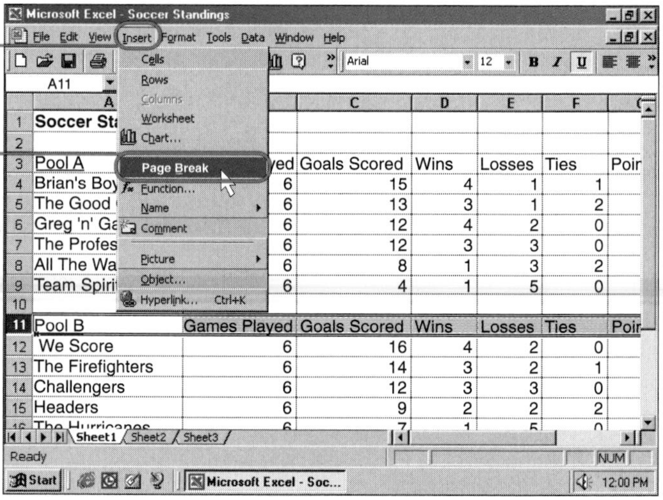

2 Click **Insert**.

3 Click **Page Break**.

*Note: If Page Break does not
appear on the menu, position
the mouse over the bottom
of the menu to display all the
menu commands.*

Point Standings

Players	Games	Goals	Assists	Points
A. Henderson	60	4	12	16
G. Hampton	60	25	12	37
J. Carnes	60	2	5	7
M. Whittaker	60	49	20	69
R. Fitzgerald	60	21	12	33
R. Johnson	60	52	24	76
R. White	60	15	23	38
S. Nurse	60	12	10	22
S. Stevenson	60	19	21	40
W. MacMillan	60	19	30	9
L. Kinnear	60	9	6	14
H. Jackson	58	14	3	
B. Sitts	59	3	4	
T. Taylor	60	10	6	
T. Kinnear	5	12	12	24

A dotted line appears on your screen. This line indicates where one page ends and another begins. The dotted line will not appear when you print your worksheet.

To deselect a row or column, click any cell.

DELETE A PAGE BREAK

1 Click a cell directly below or directly to the right of the page break line you want to delete.

2 Click **Insert**.

3 Click **Remove Page Break** to remove the page break.

The dotted line disappears from your worksheet.

VIEW ALL PAGE BREAKS

You can view all
the page breaks
in your worksheet
at once.

Page Breaks

VIEW ALL PAGE BREAKS

1 Click **View**.

2 Click **Page Break Preview** to display all the page breaks in your worksheet.

■ A Welcome dialog box appears.

3 Click **OK** to close the dialog box.

? Why do some page break lines appear dotted in Page Break Preview?

The dotted lines indicate page breaks that Excel inserted for you. Excel displays page breaks you inserted as solid lines.

Excel Breaks

Your Breaks

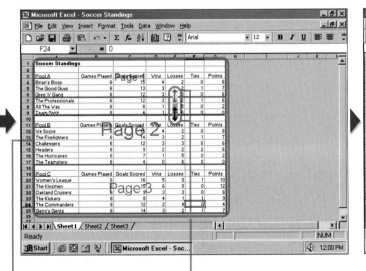

■ Blue lines show the location of the page breaks in your worksheet.

MOVE A PAGE BREAK

1 Position the mouse ⌖ over the page break line you want to move (⌖ changes to ↕ or ↔).

2 Drag the page break line to a new location.

■ The page break line appears in the new location.

RETURN TO NORMAL VIEW

1 To return to the normal view at any time, repeat steps **1** and **2** on page 182, except select **Normal** in step **2**.

ADD A HEADER OR FOOTER

You can add a header or footer to every page of your worksheet. A header or footer can contain information such as the workbook name, the page number and the current date.

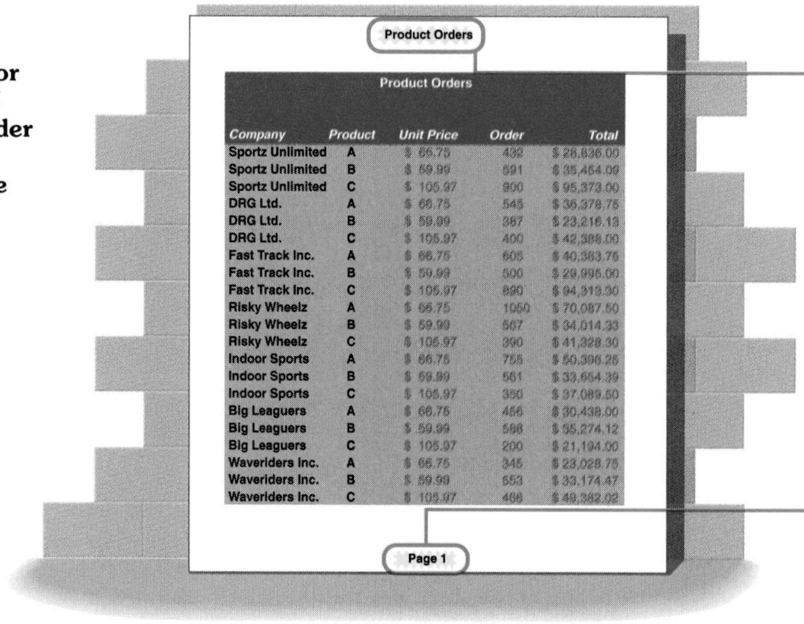

■ A **header** appears at the top of each printed page.

■ A **footer** appears at the bottom of each printed page.

ADD A HEADER OR FOOTER

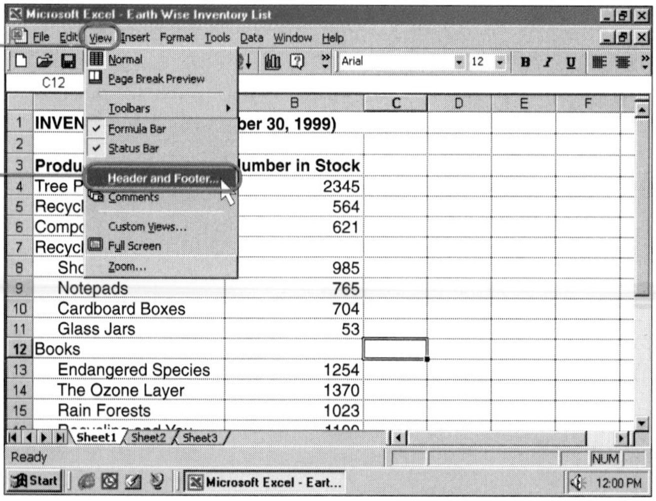

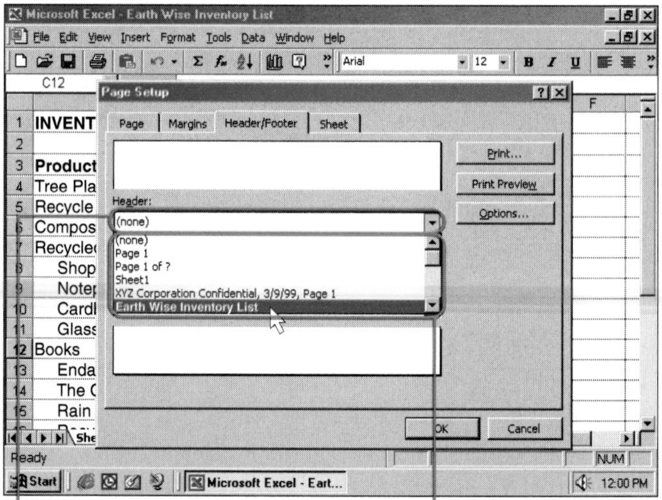

1 Click **View**.

2 Click **Header and Footer**.

Note: If Header and Footer does not appear on the menu, position the mouse over the bottom of the menu to display all the menu commands.

■ The Page Setup dialog box appears.

3 To view a list of headers you can use, click this area.

4 Click the header you want to use.

?

Can I see how a header or footer will look before I print my worksheet?

You can use the Print Preview feature to view a header or footer on your worksheet before you print the worksheet. For information on the Print Preview feature, see page 168.

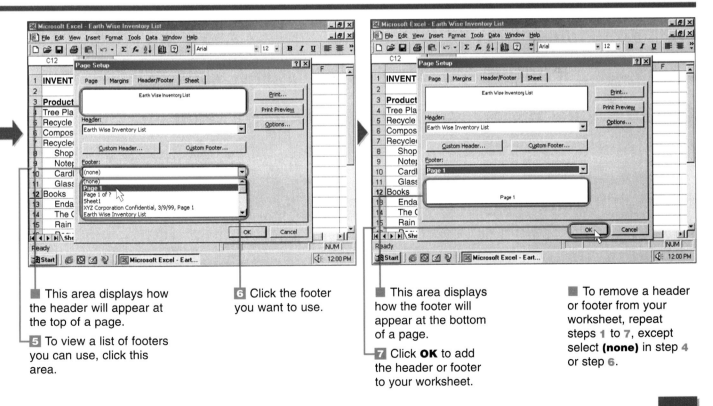

■ This area displays how the header will appear at the top of a page.

5 To view a list of footers you can use, click this area.

6 Click the footer you want to use.

■ This area displays how the footer will appear at the bottom of a page.

7 Click **OK** to add the header or footer to your worksheet.

■ To remove a header or footer from your worksheet, repeat steps **1** to **7**, except select **(none)** in step **4** or step **6**.

ADD A HEADER OR FOOTER

You can create a custom header or footer to display specific information on each printed page.

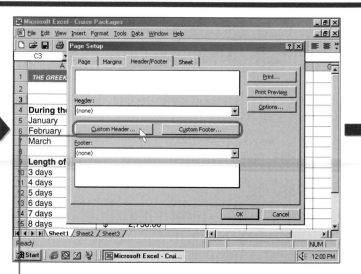

A custom header or footer could contain information such as your e-mail address.

CREATE A CUSTOM HEADER OR FOOTER

1 Click **View**.

2 Click **Header and Footer**.

Note: If Header and Footer does not appear on the menu, position the mouse ⌖ over the bottom of the menu to display all the menu commands.

■ The Page Setup dialog box appears.

3 Click the appropriate button to select whether you want to create a custom header or footer.

■ A dialog box appears, displaying areas for the left, center and right sections of the page.

?

Can Excel help me enter information into my header or footer?

You can click one of the following buttons to have Excel enter information into your header or footer.

🔢 Insert page number	🕐 Insert current time
📄 Insert total number of pages	📊 Insert workbook name
📅 Insert current date	🖥 Insert worksheet name

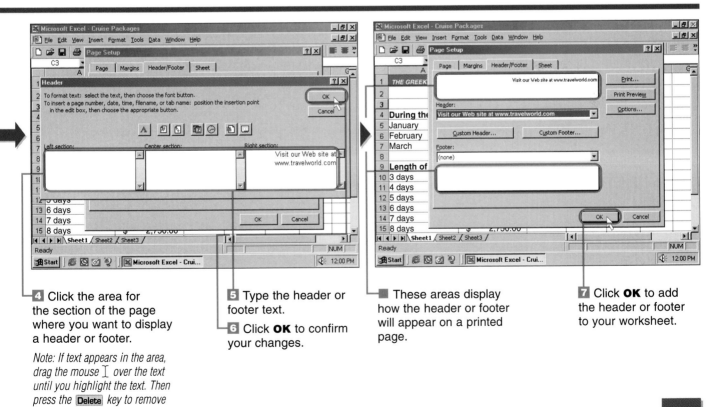

■4 Click the area for the section of the page where you want to display a header or footer.

Note: If text appears in the area, drag the mouse I over the text until you highlight the text. Then press the Delete *key to remove the text.*

■5 Type the header or footer text.

■6 Click **OK** to confirm your changes.

■ These areas display how the header or footer will appear on a printed page.

■7 Click **OK** to add the header or footer to your worksheet.

CHANGE SIZE OF PRINTED DATA

You can reduce the size of printed data to print your worksheet on a specific number of pages.

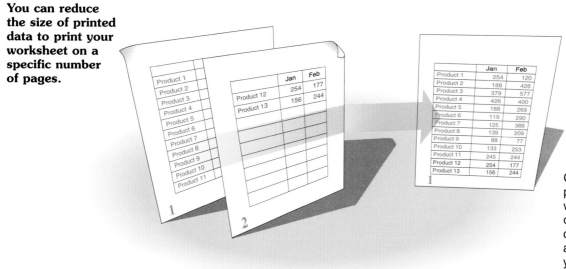

Changing the size of printed data is useful when the last page of your worksheet contains a small amount of data that you want to fit on the previous page.

1 Click **File**.

2 Click **Page Setup**.

■ The Page Setup dialog box appears.

3 Click the **Page** tab.

4 Click **Fit to** to fit the worksheet on a specific number of pages (○ changes to ◉).

?

What information does Excel require to change the size of my printed data?

To change the size of printed data, you must specify how many pages you want the data to print across and down.

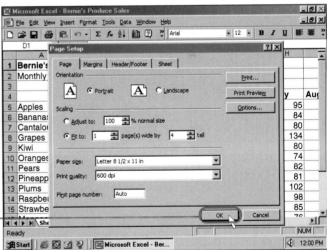

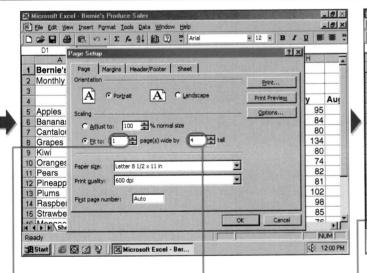

■5 Type the number of pages you want the data to print across.

■6 Press the `Tab` key and then type the number of pages you want the data to print down.

■7 Click **OK** to confirm your changes.

■ Excel will change the size of the printed data to fit on the number of pages you specified.

■ Changing the size of printed data affects the way your worksheet appears when printed, but does not affect the way the worksheet appears on your screen.

REPEAT LABELS ON PRINTED PAGES

You can display the same row or column labels on every printed page. This can help you review worksheets that print on more than one page.

REPEAT LABELS ON PRINTED PAGES

1 Click **File**.

2 Click **Page Setup**.

■ The Page Setup dialog box appears.

3 Click the **Sheet** tab.

4 Click the area beside one of these options.

Rows to repeat at top

Repeat labels across top of each page

Columns to repeat at left

Repeat labels down left side of each page

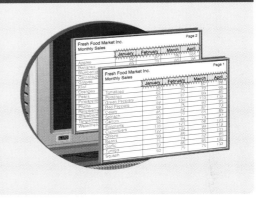

?

How can I see the repeated labels on my screen?

The repeated row or column labels will only appear when you print your worksheet. The labels will not be repeated on your screen. You can use the Print Preview feature to see how the repeated labels will look when you print your worksheet. For information on the Print Preview feature, see page 168.

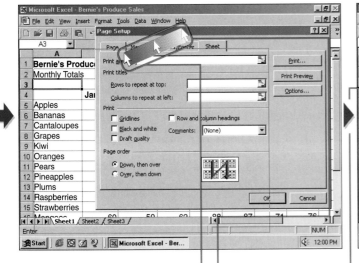

■ If the Page Setup dialog box covers the row or column containing the labels you want to repeat, you can move the dialog box to a new location.

5 To move the dialog box, position the mouse over the title bar.

6 Drag the dialog box to a new location.

7 Click one cell in the row or column containing the labels you want to repeat.

8 Click **OK** to confirm your changes.

CHAPTER 8

Work With Multiple Worksheets

Do you want to work with more than one worksheet at a time? This chapter teaches you how to switch between worksheets, move or copy data between worksheets and more.

SWITCH BETWEEN WORKSHEETS

The worksheet displayed on your screen is one of several worksheets in your workbook. You can easily switch from one worksheet to another.

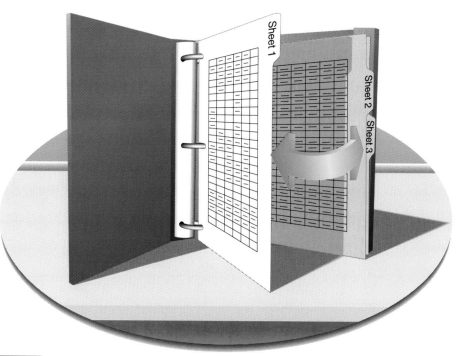

SWITCH BETWEEN WORKSHEETS

■ The worksheet currently displayed on your screen has a white tab.

■ The other worksheets in the workbook have gray tabs. The contents of these worksheets are hidden.

1 To display the contents of a worksheet, click the tab of the worksheet.

■ The contents of the worksheet appear.

■ The worksheet you selected now displays a white tab.

Why would I need more than one worksheet?

Worksheets can help you organize information in your workbook. For example, you can store information for each division of a company on a separate worksheet.

BROWSE THROUGH WORKSHEET TABS

■ If you have many worksheets in your workbook, you may not be able to see all the tabs in this area.

Note: To insert additional worksheets, see page 196.

1 Click one of these buttons to browse through the tabs.

◄ Display first tab

◄ Display tab to the left

► Display tab to the right

►| Display last tab

INSERT A WORKSHEET

You can insert a new worksheet to add related information to your workbook.

Each workbook you create automatically contains three worksheets. You can insert as many new worksheets as you need.

INSERT A WORKSHEET

1 Click the tab of the worksheet you want to appear after the new worksheet.

2 Click **Insert**.

3 Click **Worksheet**.

■ The new worksheet appears.

■ Excel displays a tab for the new worksheet.

You can permanently
remove a worksheet
you no longer need
from your workbook.

DELETE A WORKSHEET

1 Click the tab of
the worksheet you
want to delete.

2 Click **Edit**.

3 Click **Delete Sheet**.

*Note: If Delete Sheet does not
appear on the menu, position
the mouse ▷ over the bottom
of the menu to display all the
menu commands.*

■ A warning dialog box
appears.

4 Click **OK** to permanently
delete the worksheet.

RENAME A WORKSHEET

You can give each worksheet in your workbook a descriptive name. Descriptive names can help you locate information of interest.

RENAME A WORKSHEET

1 Double-click the tab of the worksheet you want to rename.

■ The current name is highlighted.

2 Type a new name and then press the **Enter** key.

Note: A worksheet name can contain up to 31 characters, including spaces.

You can reorganize
data by moving
a worksheet to a
new location in
your workbook.

MOVE A WORKSHEET

1 Position the mouse ⟍
over the tab of the
worksheet you want
to move.

2 Drag the worksheet
to a new location.

■ An arrow (▼) shows
where the worksheet
will appear.

■ The worksheet
appears in the new
location.

MOVE OR COPY DATA BETWEEN WORKSHEETS

You can move or copy data from one worksheet to another. This will save you time when you want to use data from another worksheet.

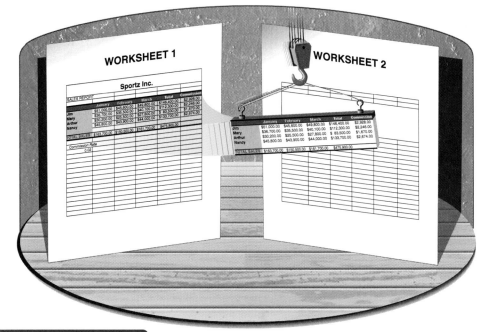

MOVE OR COPY DATA BETWEEN WORKSHEETS

1 Select the cells containing the data you want to move or copy to another worksheet. To select cells, see page 16.

2 Click one of the following buttons.

✂ Move data

📋 Copy data

Note: If the button you want is not displayed, click ⏷ on the Standard toolbar to display all the buttons.

Note: The Clipboard toolbar may appear when you move or copy data. To use the Clipboard toolbar, see page 57.

What is the difference between moving and copying data?

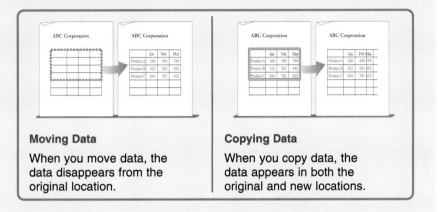

Moving Data

When you move data, the data disappears from the original location.

Copying Data

When you copy data, the data appears in both the original and new locations.

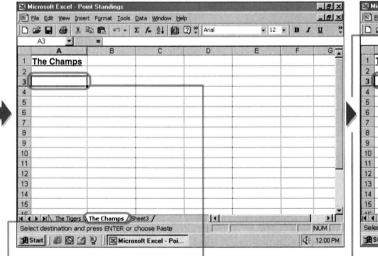

3 Click the tab of the worksheet where you want to place the data.

Note: To place the data in another workbook, open the workbook before performing step 3. To open a workbook, see page 38.

4 Click the cell where you want to place the data. This cell will become the top left cell of the new location.

5 Click 🖻 to place the data in the new location.

Note: If 🖻 is not displayed, click 🔽 on the Standard toolbar to display all the buttons.

■ The data appears in the new location.

Note: If number signs (#) appear in a cell, the column is too narrow to fit the data. To change the column width, see page 68.

ENTER A FORMULA ACROSS WORKSHEETS

You can enter a formula in one worksheet that uses data from other worksheets.

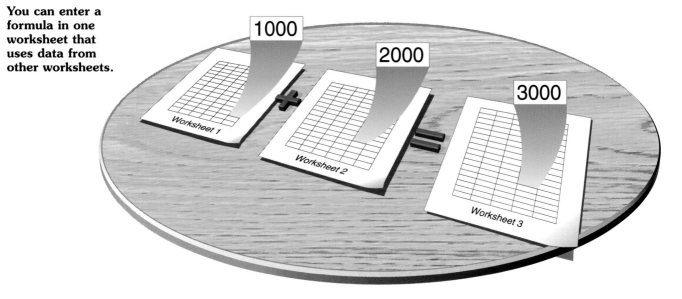

1 To select the cell where you want to enter a formula, click the cell.

2 Type an equal sign (=) to begin the formula.

3 Click the tab of the worksheet containing the data you want to use in the formula.

■ The worksheet appears.

4 Click a cell containing data you want to use in the formula.

5 Type the symbol for the calculation you want to perform, such as + or *.

What happens if I change a number used in a formula?

If you change a number used in a formula, Excel will automatically calculate a new result. This ensures that your calculations are always up-to-date.

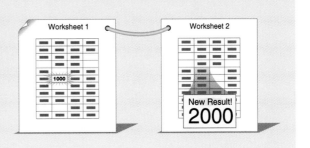

6 Repeat steps **3** to **5** until you have selected all the cells containing data you want to use in the formula.

*Note: In this example, cells **B4** to **B7** are added together.*

7 Press the Enter key to complete the formula.

■ The result of the calculation appears in the cell you selected in step **1**.

8 To view the formula you entered, click the cell containing the formula.

■ The formula bar displays the worksheet name and cell reference for each cell used in the formula.

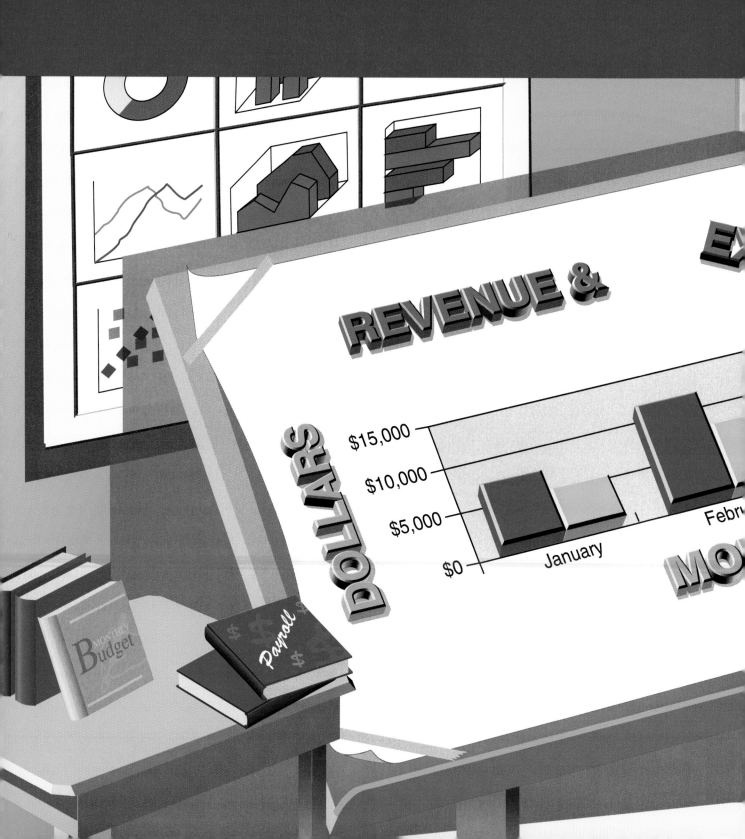

CHAPTER 9

Work With Charts

Are you interested in displaying your worksheet data in a chart? In this chapter you will learn how to create, change and print charts.

INTRODUCTION TO CHARTS

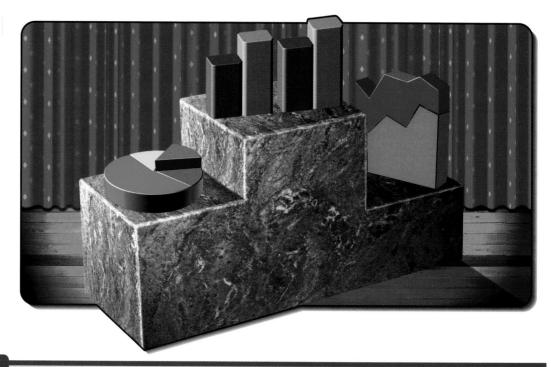

A chart allows you to visually display your worksheet data. Excel offers many different chart types.

PARTS OF A CHART

Data Series

A group of related data representing one row or column from your worksheet. Each data series is represented by a specific color, pattern or symbol.

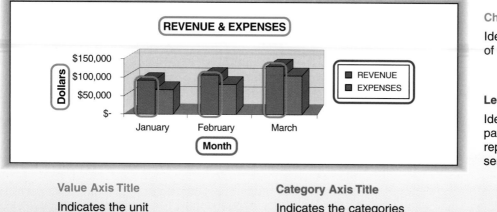

Chart Title

Identifies the subject of your chart.

Legend

Identifies the color, pattern or symbol that represents each data series in your chart.

Value Axis Title

Indicates the unit of measure used in your chart.

Category Axis Title

Indicates the categories used in your chart.

COMMON CHART TYPES

Area

An area chart is useful for showing the amount of change in data over time. Each line represents a data series.

Line

A line chart is useful for showing changes to data at regular intervals. Each line represents a data series.

Column

A column chart is useful for showing changes to data over time or comparing individual items. Each column represents an item in a data series.

Bar

A bar chart is useful for comparing individual items. Each bar represents an item in a data series.

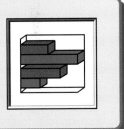

Pie

A pie chart is useful for showing the relationship of parts to a whole. Each piece of a pie represents an item in a data series. A pie chart can show only one data series at a time.

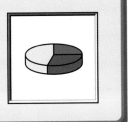

Doughnut

A doughnut chart is useful for showing the relationship of parts to a whole. Unlike a pie chart, a doughnut chart can display more than one data series. Each ring represents a data series.

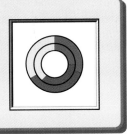

Radar

A radar chart is useful for comparing the items in several data series. Each data series is shown as a line around a central point.

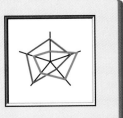

XY (Scatter)

An xy (scatter) chart is useful for showing the relationship between two or more data series measured at uneven intervals.

CREATE A CHART

You can create a chart to graphically display your worksheet data.

CREATE A CHART

1 Select the cells containing the data you want to display in a chart, including the row and column labels. To select cells, see page 16.

2 Click 📊 to create the chart.

Note: If 📊 is not displayed, click 📋 on the Standard toolbar to display all the buttons.

■ The Chart Wizard appears.

3 Click the type of chart you want to create.

4 Click the chart design you want to use.

Note: The available chart designs depend on the type of chart you selected in step 3.

5 Click **Next** to continue.

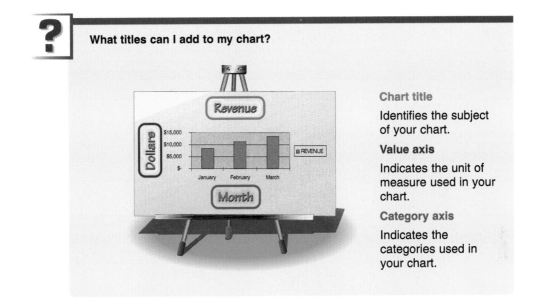

What titles can I add to my chart?

Chart title

Identifies the subject of your chart.

Value axis

Indicates the unit of measure used in your chart.

Category axis

Indicates the categories used in your chart.

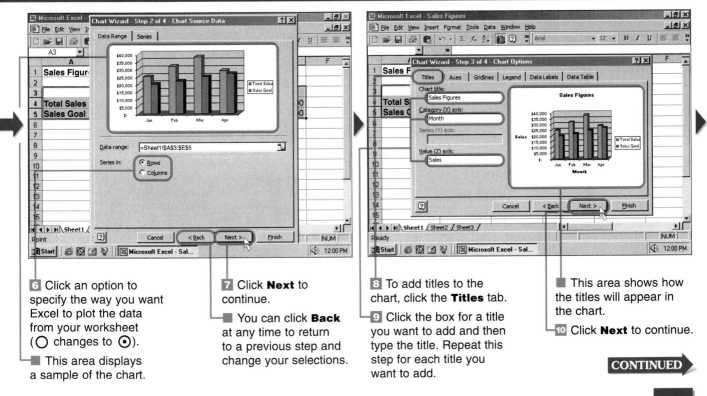

6 Click an option to specify the way you want Excel to plot the data from your worksheet (◯ changes to ⦿).

■ This area displays a sample of the chart.

7 Click **Next** to continue.

■ You can click **Back** at any time to return to a previous step and change your selections.

8 To add titles to the chart, click the **Titles** tab.

9 Click the box for a title you want to add and then type the title. Repeat this step for each title you want to add.

■ This area shows how the titles will appear in the chart.

10 Click **Next** to continue.

CONTINUED ▶

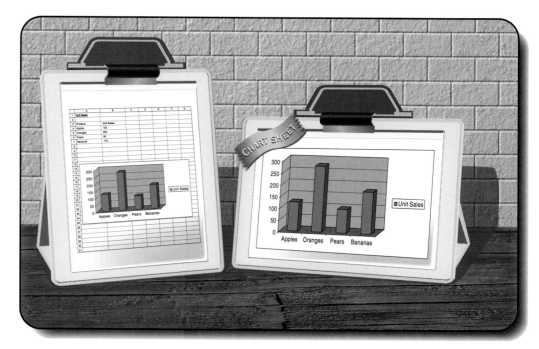

When creating a chart, you can choose to display the chart on the same worksheet as the data or on its own sheet, called a chart sheet.

CREATE A CHART (CONTINUED)

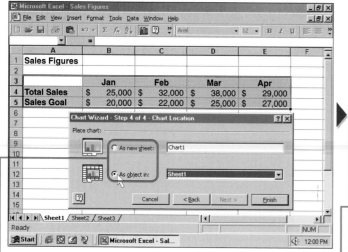

■ Click an option to specify where you want to display the chart (○ changes to ⊙).

As new sheet
Display chart on its own sheet, called a chart sheet

As object in
Display chart on the same worksheet as the data

■ Click **Finish** to complete the chart.

Do I have to create a new chart each time I change data in my worksheet?

No. When you edit the data you used to create the chart, Excel will automatically update the chart to display the changes.

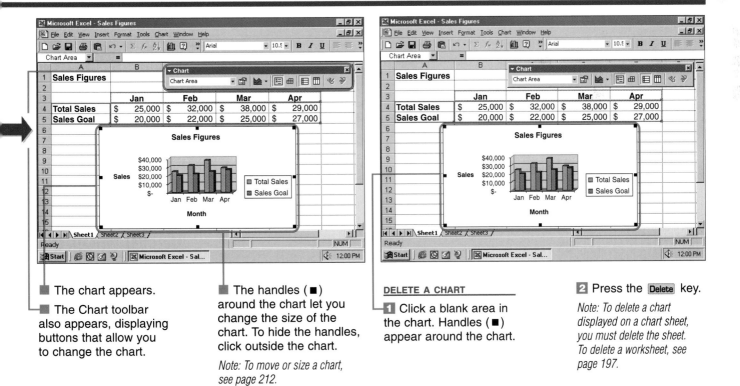

■ The chart appears.

■ The Chart toolbar also appears, displaying buttons that allow you to change the chart.

■ The handles (■) around the chart let you change the size of the chart. To hide the handles, click outside the chart.

Note: To move or size a chart, see page 212.

DELETE A CHART

1 Click a blank area in the chart. Handles (■) appear around the chart.

2 Press the Delete key.

Note: To delete a chart displayed on a chart sheet, you must delete the sheet. To delete a worksheet, see page 197.

MOVE OR SIZE A CHART

After you create a chart, you can change the location or size of the chart.

MOVE A CHART

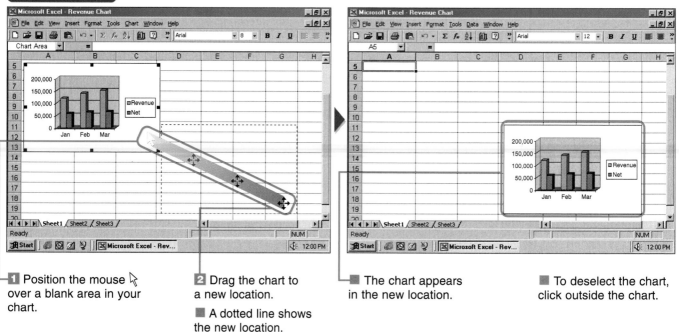

1 Position the mouse ⌖ over a blank area in your chart.

2 Drag the chart to a new location.

■ A dotted line shows the new location.

■ The chart appears in the new location.

■ To deselect the chart, click outside the chart.

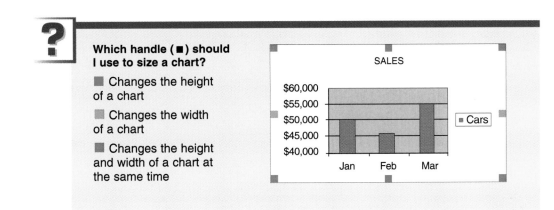

Which handle (■) should I use to size a chart?

■ Changes the height of a chart

■ Changes the width of a chart

■ Changes the height and width of a chart at the same time

SIZE A CHART

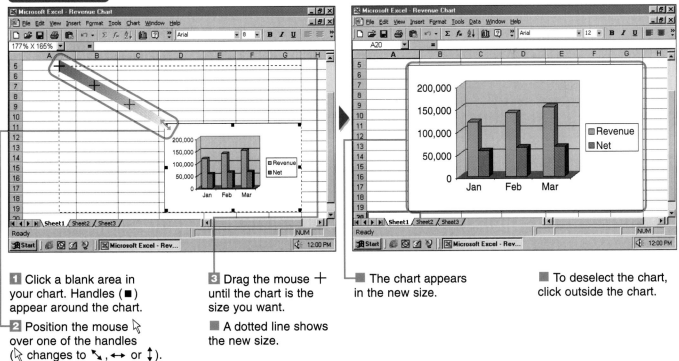

1 Click a blank area in your chart. Handles (■) appear around the chart.

2 Position the mouse 🔓 over one of the handles (🔓 changes to ↖, ↔ or ↕).

3 Drag the mouse + until the chart is the size you want.

■ A dotted line shows the new size.

■ The chart appears in the new size.

■ To deselect the chart, click outside the chart.

PRINT A CHART

You can print
your chart with
the worksheet
data or on its
own page.

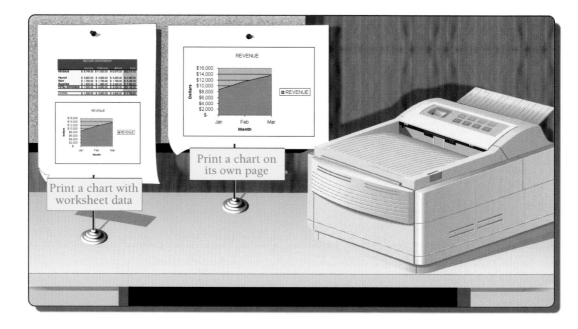

Print a chart with
worksheet data

Print a chart on
its own page

1 Click a cell outside
the chart.

2 Click 🖨 to print
the chart with your
worksheet data.

*Note: If 🖨 is not displayed,
click 》 on the Standard toolbar
to display all the buttons.*

■ The chart prints with
the worksheet data.

? Can I see how my chart will look when printed?

You can preview your chart to see how the chart will look when printed. This lets you confirm that the chart will print the way you want. For information on using the Print Preview feature, see page 168.

PRINT A CHART ON ITS OWN PAGE

1 To print a chart displayed on a worksheet, click a blank area in the chart.

■ To print a chart displayed on a chart sheet, click the tab for the chart sheet.

2 Click 🖨 to print the chart on its own page.

Note: If 🖨 is not displayed, click 🔸 on the Standard toolbar to display all the buttons.

■ When you print a chart on its own page, the chart expands to fill the page. The printed chart may look different from the chart on your screen.

CHANGE CHART TYPE

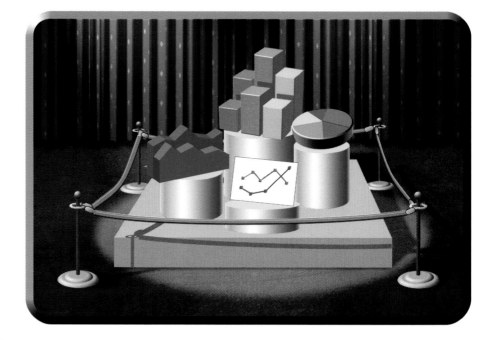

After you create a chart, you can select a different type of chart that will better suit your data.

CHANGE CHART TYPE

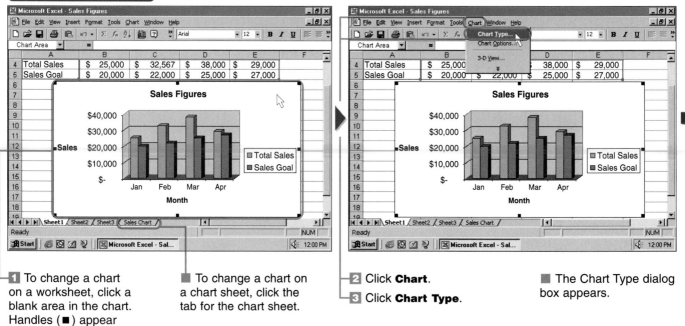

1 To change a chart on a worksheet, click a blank area in the chart. Handles (■) appear around the chart.

■ To change a chart on a chart sheet, click the tab for the chart sheet.

2 Click **Chart**.

3 Click **Chart Type**.

■ The Chart Type dialog box appears.

What type of chart should I choose?

The type of chart you should choose depends on your data. Each chart type presents data in a specific way. For example, area, column and line charts are ideal for showing changes to values over time. Pie charts are ideal for showing percentages.

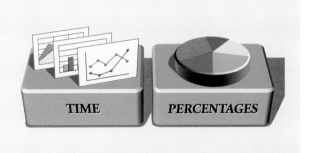

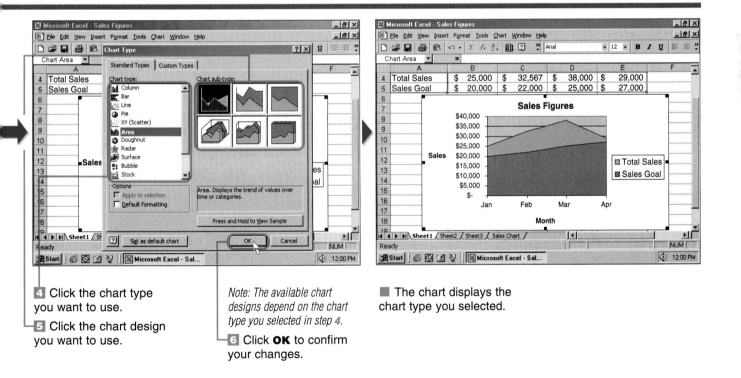

4 Click the chart type you want to use.

5 Click the chart design you want to use.

Note: The available chart designs depend on the chart type you selected in step 4.

6 Click **OK** to confirm your changes.

■ The chart displays the chart type you selected.

CHANGE CHART TITLES

You can change the titles in your chart to make the titles more meaningful.

CHANGE CHART TITLES

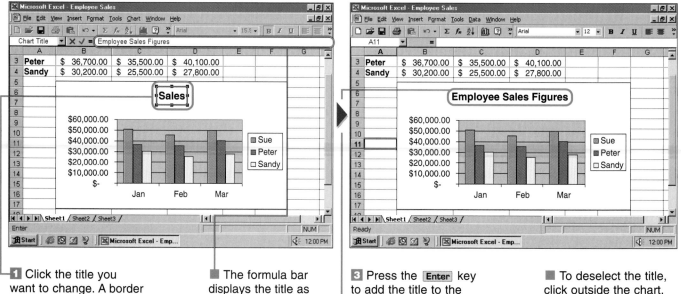

■ **1** Click the title you want to change. A border appears around the title.

■ **2** Type the new title.

■ The formula bar displays the title as you type.

■ **3** Press the **Enter** key to add the title to the chart.

■ The chart displays the new title.

■ To deselect the title, click outside the chart.

You can rotate
text on a chart
axis to improve
the appearance
of the chart.

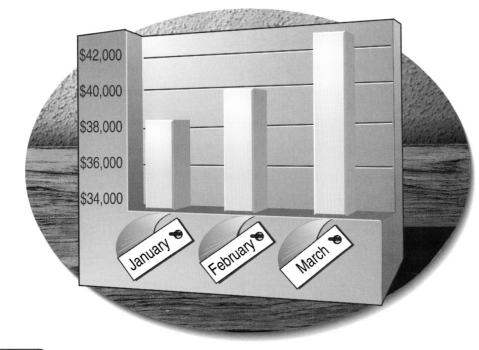

ROTATE CHART TEXT

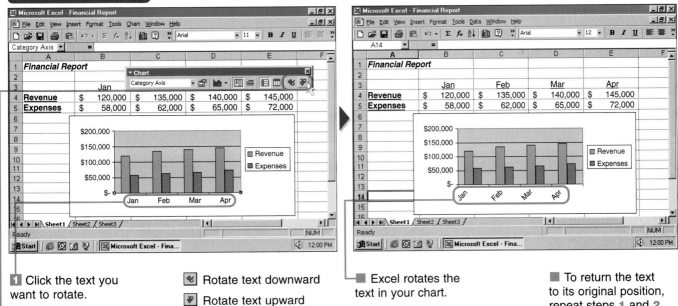

1 Click the text you
want to rotate.

2 Click one of these
buttons.

Rotate text downward

Rotate text upward

*Note: If the Chart toolbar is
not displayed, see page 118
to display the toolbar.*

■ Excel rotates the
text in your chart.

■ To deselect the text,
click outside the chart.

■ To return the text
to its original position,
repeat steps **1** and **2**.

FORMAT CHART TEXT

You can change the appearance of the text and numbers in a chart.

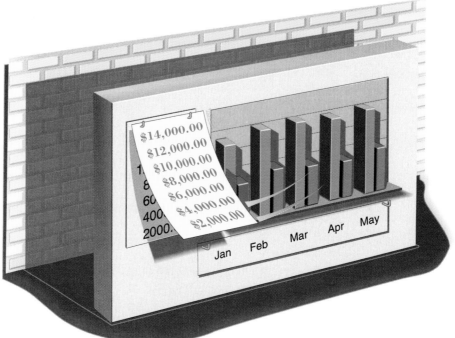

FORMAT CHART TEXT

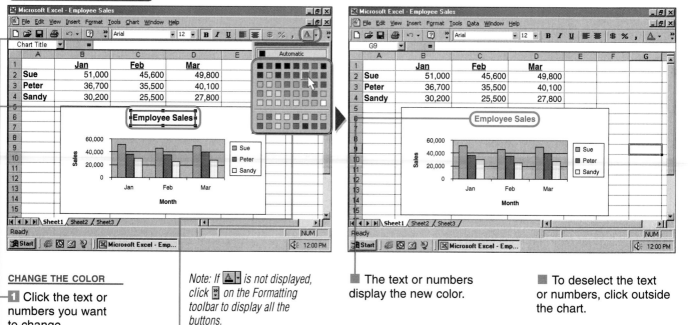

CHANGE THE COLOR

1 Click the text or numbers you want to change.

2 Click █ in this area to select a color.

Note: If ▲▾ is not displayed, click ⟫ on the Formatting toolbar to display all the buttons.

3 Click the color you want to use.

■ The text or numbers display the new color.

■ To deselect the text or numbers, click outside the chart.

220

How else can I change the appearance of the text and numbers in a chart?

Change the Font

Click the text or numbers you want to change and then perform steps **2** and **3** on page 134.

Change the Font Size

Click the text or numbers you want to change and then perform steps **2** and **3** on page 135.

Add or Remove Decimal Places from Numbers

Click the numbers you want to change and then perform step **2** on page 157.

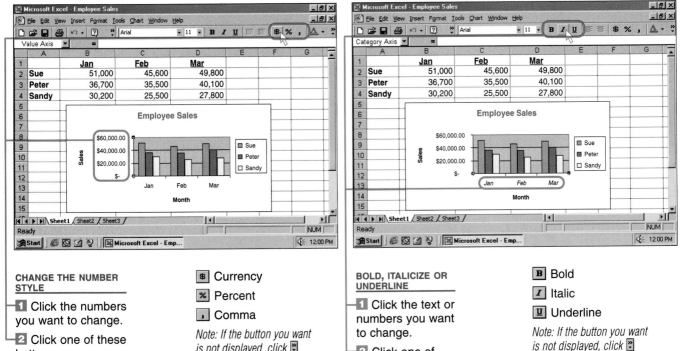

CHANGE THE NUMBER STYLE

1 Click the numbers you want to change.

2 Click one of these buttons.

$ Currency

% Percent

, Comma

Note: If the button you want is not displayed, click ▪ *on the Formatting toolbar to display all the buttons.*

BOLD, ITALICIZE OR UNDERLINE

1 Click the text or numbers you want to change.

2 Click one of these buttons.

B Bold

I Italic

U Underline

Note: If the button you want is not displayed, click ▪ *on the Formatting toolbar to display all the buttons.*

ADD DATA TO A CHART

After you create a chart, you can add new data to the chart.

Adding data to a chart is useful when you need to update the chart. For example, you can add the latest sales figures to your chart at the end of each month.

ADD DATA TO A CHART

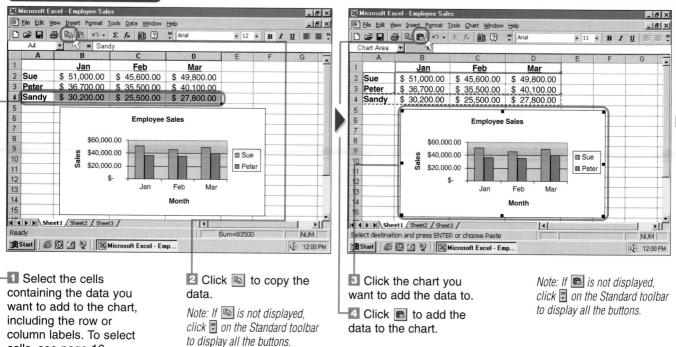

1 Select the cells containing the data you want to add to the chart, including the row or column labels. To select cells, see page 16.

2 Click 📋 to copy the data.

Note: If 📋 is not displayed, click ⏷ on the Standard toolbar to display all the buttons.

3 Click the chart you want to add the data to.

4 Click 📋 to add the data to the chart.

Note: If 📋 is not displayed, click ⏷ on the Standard toolbar to display all the buttons.

?

Can I add a data series to a pie chart?

A pie chart can display only one data series. You cannot add another data series to a pie chart.

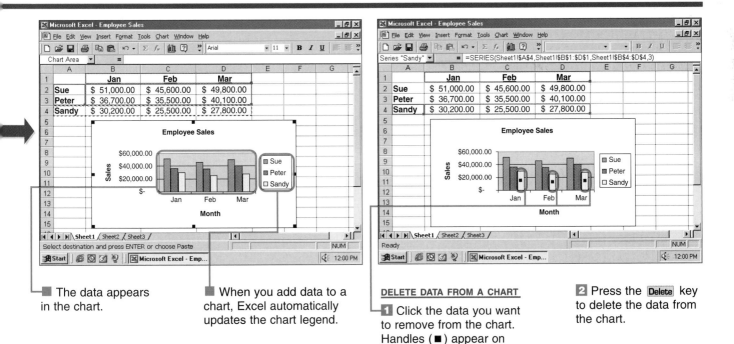

■ The data appears in the chart.

■ When you add data to a chart, Excel automatically updates the chart legend.

DELETE DATA FROM A CHART

1 Click the data you want to remove from the chart. Handles (■) appear on the data series.

2 Press the Delete key to delete the data from the chart.

ADD A DATA TABLE TO A CHART

You can add a table to your chart to display the data used to create the chart.

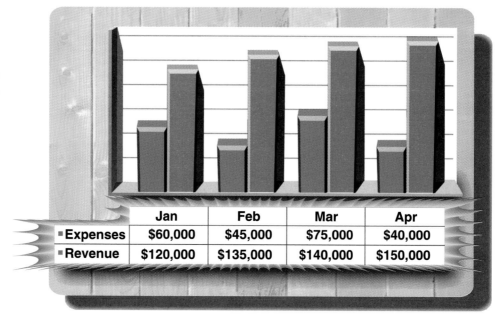

	Jan	Feb	Mar	Apr
▪ **Expenses**	**$60,000**	**$45,000**	**$75,000**	**$40,000**
▪ **Revenue**	**$120,000**	**$135,000**	**$140,000**	**$150,000**

ADD A DATA TABLE TO A CHART

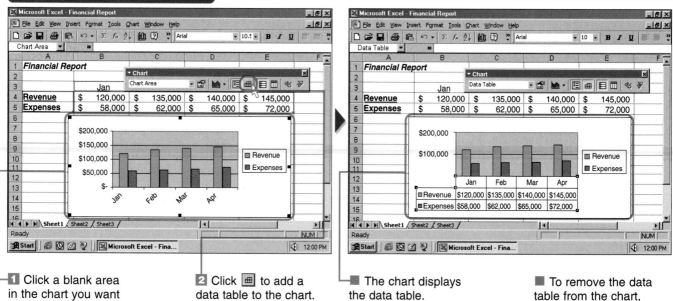

1 Click a blank area in the chart you want to change.

Note: You cannot add a data table to some types of charts.

2 Click ⊞ to add a data table to the chart.

Note: If the Chart toolbar is not displayed, see page 118 to display the toolbar.

■ The chart displays the data table.

■ To remove the data table from the chart, repeat steps **1** and **2**.

CHANGE THE WAY DATA IS PLOTTED

You can change the way Excel plots the data in your chart. This allows you to emphasize different information in the chart.

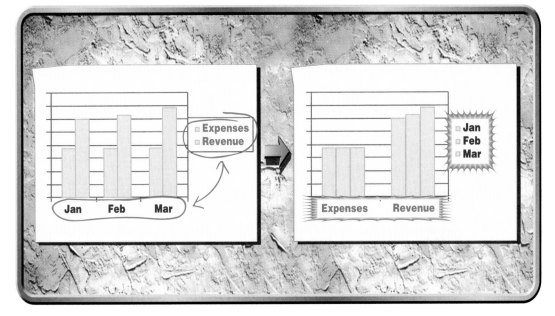

CHANGE THE WAY DATA IS PLOTTED

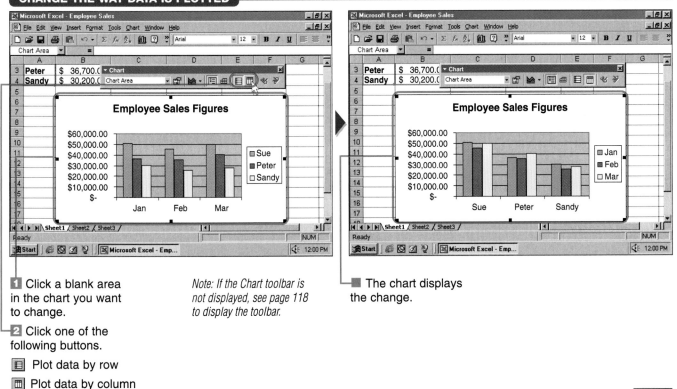

1 Click a blank area in the chart you want to change.

2 Click one of the following buttons.

▦ Plot data by row

▥ Plot data by column

Note: If the Chart toolbar is not displayed, see page 118 to display the toolbar.

■ The chart displays the change.

CHANGE APPEARANCE OF DATA SERIES

You can change the color of a data series in a chart. You can also add a pattern to a data series.

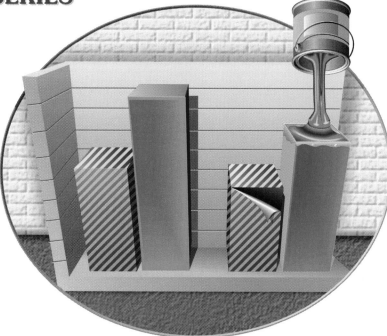

If you are printing your chart on a black-and-white printer, adding a pattern to a data series may make it easier to identify the data series in the chart.

CHANGE COLOR OF DATA SERIES

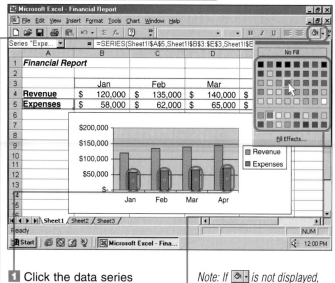

1 Click the data series you want to change. Handles (■) appear on the data series.

2 Click ∵ in this area to select a color for the data series.

Note: If ◇ ∵ is not displayed, click » on the Formatting toolbar to display all the buttons.

3 Click the color you want to use.

■ The data series displays the new color.

ADD PATTERN TO DATA SERIES

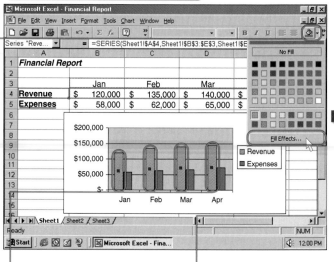

1 Click the data series you want to change. Handles (■) appear on the data series.

2 Click ∵ in this area.

Note: If ◇ ∵ is not displayed, click » on the Formatting toolbar to display all the buttons.

3 Click **Fill Effects**.

■ The Fill Effects dialog box appears.

Can I change the color of other parts of a chart?

You can change the color of other parts of a chart, such as the background of the chart or the chart legend. Click the part of the chart you want to change and then perform steps **2** and **3** on page 226 to select the color you want to use.

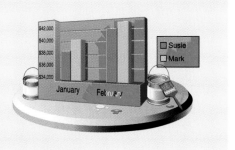

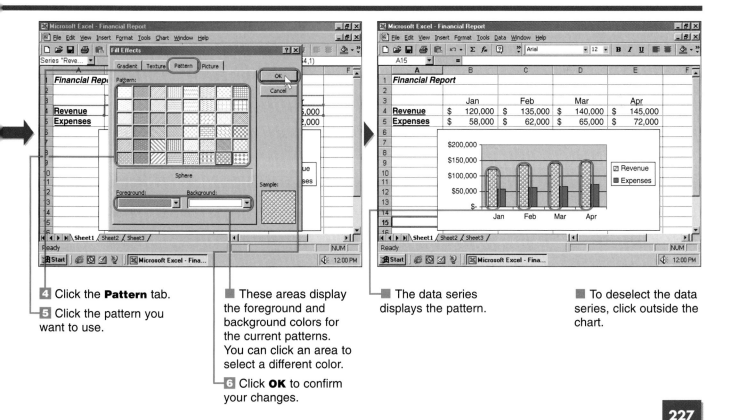

4 Click the **Pattern** tab.

5 Click the pattern you want to use.

■ These areas display the foreground and background colors for the current patterns. You can click an area to select a different color.

6 Click **OK** to confirm your changes.

■ The data series displays the pattern.

■ To deselect the data series, click outside the chart.

CHANGE VIEW OF A 3-D CHART

You can change the elevation, rotation and perspective of a 3-D chart. This can help you emphasize the important parts of your chart.

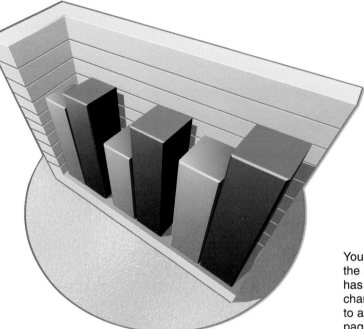

You can only change the 3-D view if the chart has a 3-D design. To change the chart type to a 3-D design, see page 216.

CHANGE VIEW OF A 3-D CHART

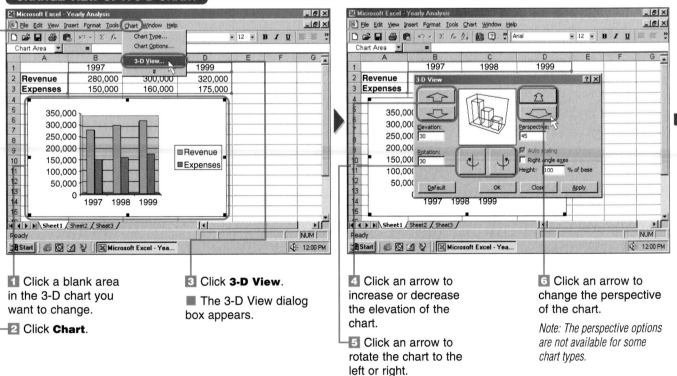

1 Click a blank area in the 3-D chart you want to change.

2 Click **Chart**.

3 Click **3-D View**.

■ The 3-D View dialog box appears.

4 Click an arrow to increase or decrease the elevation of the chart.

5 Click an arrow to rotate the chart to the left or right.

6 Click an arrow to change the perspective of the chart.

Note: The perspective options are not available for some chart types.

What is the difference between elevation, rotation and perspective?

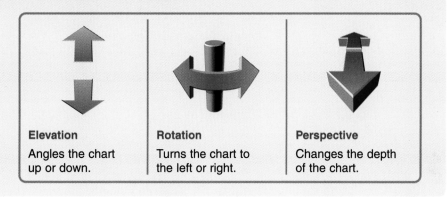

Elevation
Angles the chart up or down.

Rotation
Turns the chart to the left or right.

Perspective
Changes the depth of the chart.

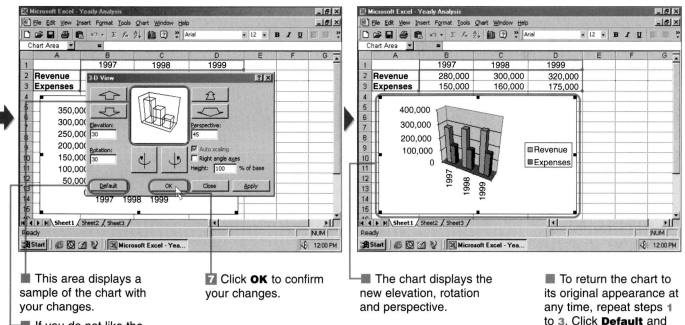

■ This area displays a sample of the chart with your changes.

■ If you do not like the changes, click **Default** to undo all your changes.

7 Click **OK** to confirm your changes.

■ The chart displays the new elevation, rotation and perspective.

■ To return the chart to its original appearance at any time, repeat steps **1** to **3**. Click **Default** and then perform step **7**.

CHAPTER 10

Work With Graphics

Are you wondering how to use graphics to enhance the appearance of your worksheet? This chapter shows you how.

ADD AN AUTOSHAPE

Excel provides many ready-made shapes, called AutoShapes, that you can add to your worksheet or chart.

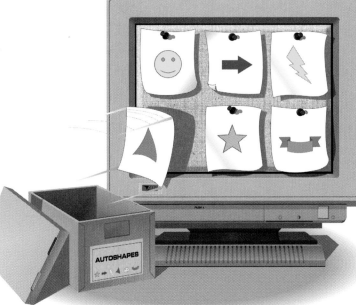

AutoShapes can help illustrate information or draw attention to important data in your worksheet.

ADD AN AUTOSHAPE

1 To add an AutoShape to your worksheet, click a cell in the worksheet.

■ To add an AutoShape to a chart, click the chart.

2 Click 🖉 to display the Drawing toolbar.

Note: If 🖉 is not displayed, click 📄 on the Standard toolbar to display all the buttons.

■ The Drawing toolbar appears.

3 Click **AutoShapes**.

4 Click the type of AutoShape you want to add.

Note: If the type of AutoShape you want does not appear on the menu, position the mouse ⫿ over the bottom of the menu to display all the menu commands.

5 Click the AutoShape you want to add.

?

Can I add text to an AutoShape?

You can add text to most AutoShapes. This is particularly useful for AutoShapes such as banners. To add text to an AutoShape, click the AutoShape and then type the text you want the AutoShape to display.

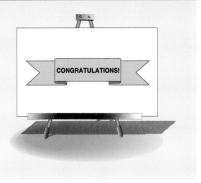

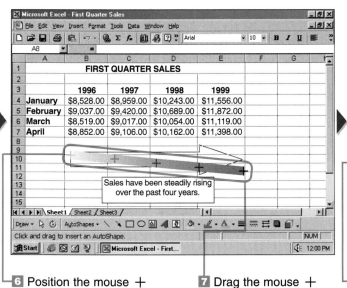

6 Position the mouse + where you want to begin drawing the AutoShape.

7 Drag the mouse + until the AutoShape is the size you want.

■ The AutoShape appears. The handles (□) around the AutoShape let you change the size of the AutoShape. To move or size an AutoShape, see page 242.

8 To hide the handles, click outside the AutoShape.

Note: To hide the Drawing toolbar, repeat step 2.

DELETE AN AUTOSHAPE

1 Click an edge of the AutoShape you want to delete. Then press the `Delete` key.

You can use the
WordArt feature
to add a text
effect to your
worksheet or
chart.

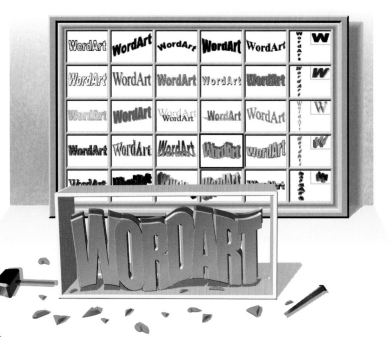

Adding a text effect is
an easy way to create
an eye-catching title.

ADD A TEXT EFFECT

1 To add a text effect
to your worksheet, click
a cell in the worksheet.

■ To add a text effect
to a chart, click the chart.

2 Click 🖼 to display
the Drawing toolbar.

*Note: If 🖼 is not displayed,
click 📄 on the Standard toolbar
to display all the buttons.*

■ The Drawing toolbar
appears.

3 Click 🔷 to add
a text effect.

■ The WordArt Gallery
dialog box appears.

4 Click the type of text
effect you want to add.

5 Click **OK** to confirm
your selection.

How do I edit a text effect?

Double-click the text effect to display the Edit WordArt Text dialog box. Then edit the text in the dialog box. When you finish editing the text effect, click **OK**.

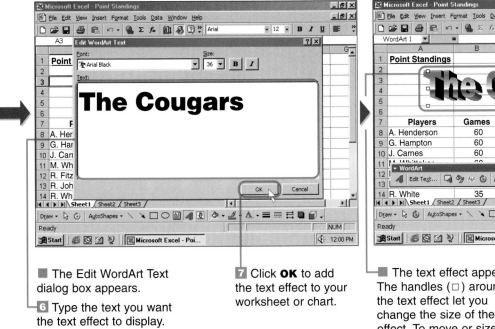

■ The Edit WordArt Text dialog box appears.

6 Type the text you want the text effect to display.

7 Click **OK** to add the text effect to your worksheet or chart.

■ The text effect appears. The handles (□) around the text effect let you change the size of the text effect. To move or size a text effect, see page 242.

8 To hide the handles, click outside the text effect.

Note: To hide the Drawing toolbar, repeat step 2.

DELETE A TEXT EFFECT

1 Click the text effect you want to delete. Then press the Delete key.

ADD A TEXT BOX

You can add a text box to your worksheet or chart to display additional information.

Text boxes are useful for displaying notes. You can also use text boxes to label or describe items in your worksheet or chart.

ADD A TEXT BOX

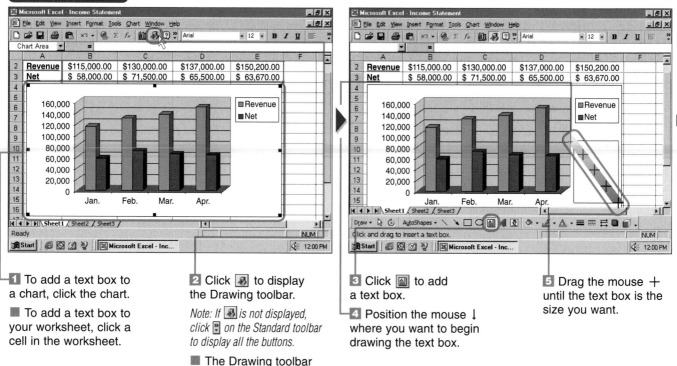

1 To add a text box to a chart, click the chart.

■ To add a text box to your worksheet, click a cell in the worksheet.

2 Click 🖋 to display the Drawing toolbar.

Note: If 🖋 is not displayed, click 🔽 on the Standard toolbar to display all the buttons.

■ The Drawing toolbar appears.

3 Click 📰 to add a text box.

4 Position the mouse ↓ where you want to begin drawing the text box.

5 Drag the mouse ✛ until the text box is the size you want.

236

How do I edit the text in a text box?

To edit the text, click the text box and then edit the text as you would edit any text in your worksheet. When you finish editing the text, click outside the text box.

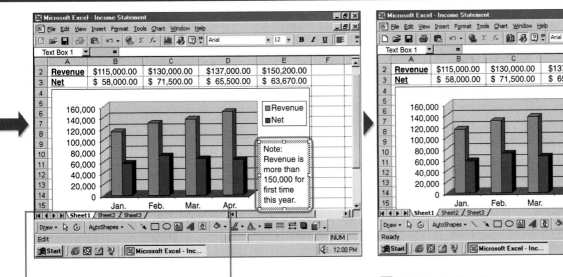

■ The text box appears.

6 Type the text you want the text box to display.

■ The handles (□) around the text box let you change the size of the text box. To move or size a text box, see page 242.

7 To hide the handles, click outside the text box.

Note: To hide the Drawing toolbar, repeat step 2.

DELETE A TEXT BOX

1 Click the text box you want to delete.

2 Click an edge of the text box and then press the Delete key.

ADD CLIP ART

Excel includes professionally designed clip art images that you can add to your worksheet or chart. Clip art images can help illustrate concepts and make your worksheet more interesting.

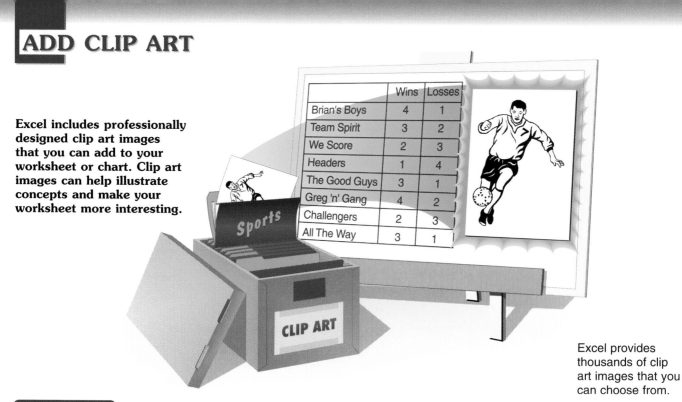

Excel provides thousands of clip art images that you can choose from.

ADD CLIP ART

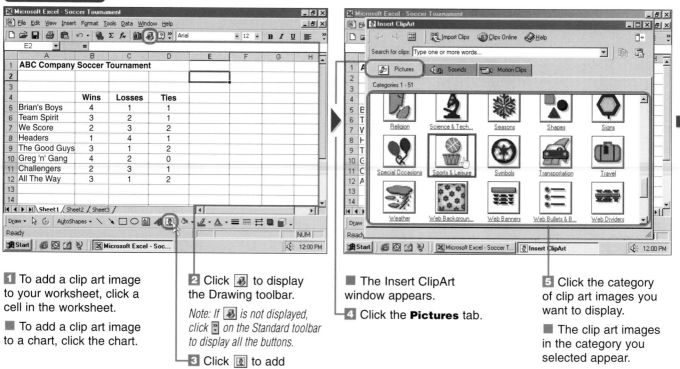

1 To add a clip art image to your worksheet, click a cell in the worksheet.

■ To add a clip art image to a chart, click the chart.

2 Click 🔲 to display the Drawing toolbar.

Note: If 🔲 is not displayed, click 🔲 on the Standard toolbar to display all the buttons.

3 Click 🔲 to add a clip art image.

■ The Insert ClipArt window appears.

4 Click the **Pictures** tab.

5 Click the category of clip art images you want to display.

■ The clip art images in the category you selected appear.

238

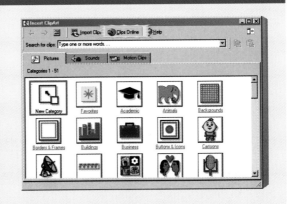

Where can I find more clip art images?

If you are connected to the Internet, you can visit Microsoft's Clip Gallery Live Web site to find additional clip art images. In the Insert ClipArt window, click **Clips Online**. In the dialog box that appears, click **OK** to connect to the Web site.

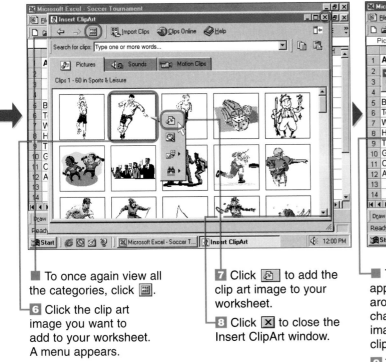

■ To once again view all the categories, click 🏢.

6 Click the clip art image you want to add to your worksheet. A menu appears.

7 Click 📷 to add the clip art image to your worksheet.

8 Click ✕ to close the Insert ClipArt window.

■ The clip art image appears. The handles (□) around the image let you change the size of the image. To move or size a clip art image, see page 242.

9 To hide the handles, click outside the clip art image.

Note: To hide the Drawing toolbar, repeat step 2.

DELETE A CLIP ART IMAGE

1 Click the clip art image you want to delete. Then press the Delete key.

ADD A PICTURE

You can add a
picture stored on
your computer to
your worksheet
or chart.

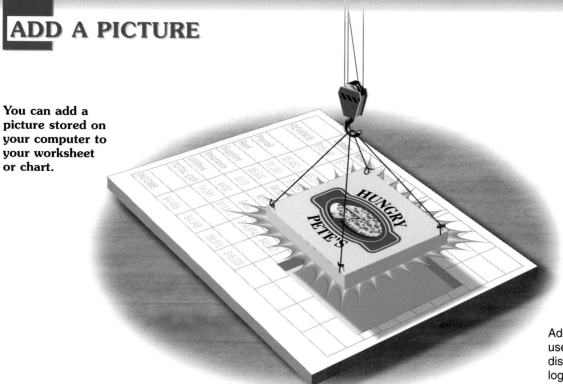

Adding a picture is
useful if you want to
display your company
logo or a picture of
your products.

ADD A PICTURE

1 To add a picture to
your worksheet, click
a cell in the worksheet.

■ To add a picture to
a chart, click the chart.

2 Click **Insert**.

3 Click **Picture**.

4 Click **From File**.

■ The Insert Picture
dialog box appears.

■ This area shows the
location of the displayed
files. You can click this
area to change the
location.

■ This area allows you
to access commonly
used folders. To display
the contents of a folder,
click the folder.

*Note: For information on the
commonly used folders, see
the top of page 29.*

Where can I get pictures that I can use in my worksheets?

You can use a drawing program to create your own pictures or use a scanner to scan pictures into your computer. You can also find collections of pictures at most computer stores and on the Internet.

5 Click the name of the picture you want to add.

■ This area displays a preview of the picture you selected.

6 Click **Insert** to add the picture to your worksheet.

■ The picture appears. The handles (□) around the picture let you change the size of the picture. To move or size a picture, see page 242.

7 To hide the handles, click outside the picture.

DELETE A PICTURE

1 Click the picture you want to delete. Then press the Delete key.

MOVE OR SIZE A GRAPHIC

You can change
the location or
size of a graphic
in your worksheet.

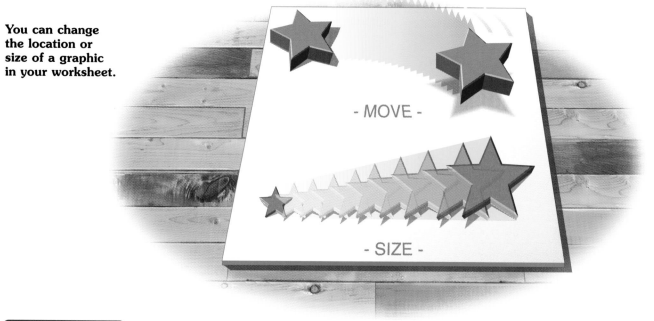

- MOVE -

- SIZE -

MOVE A GRAPHIC

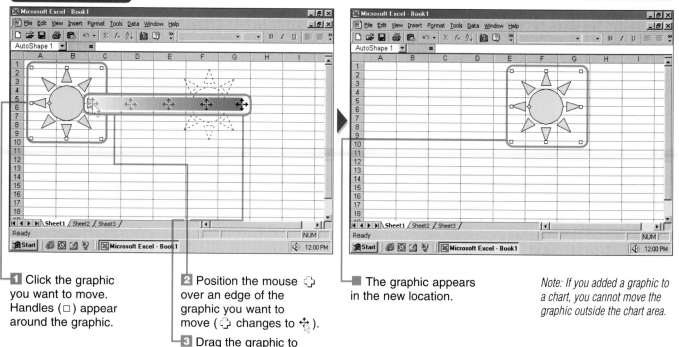

■1 Click the graphic
you want to move.
Handles (□) appear
around the graphic.

■2 Position the mouse ⊹
over an edge of the
graphic you want to
move (⊹ changes to ✥).

■3 Drag the graphic to
a new location.

■ The graphic appears
in the new location.

*Note: If you added a graphic to
a chart, you cannot move the
graphic outside the chart area.*

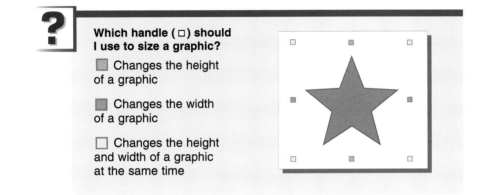

Which handle (□) should I use to size a graphic?

■ Changes the height of a graphic

■ Changes the width of a graphic

□ Changes the height and width of a graphic at the same time

SIZE A GRAPHIC

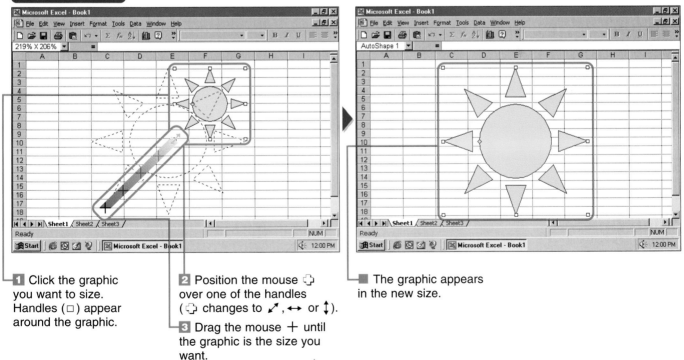

1 Click the graphic you want to size. Handles (□) appear around the graphic.

2 Position the mouse ⊕ over one of the handles (⊕ changes to ↗, ↔ or ↕).

3 Drag the mouse + until the graphic is the size you want.

■ The graphic appears in the new size.

CHANGE COLOR OF A GRAPHIC

You can change the
color of a graphic
in your worksheet
or chart.

CHANGE COLOR OF A GRAPHIC

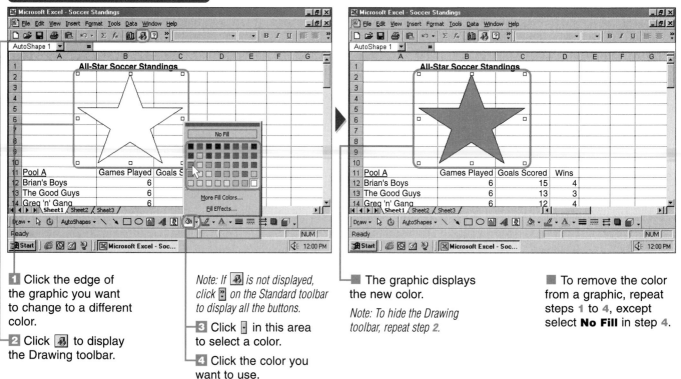

1 Click the edge of
the graphic you want
to change to a different
color.

2 Click ⬛ to display
the Drawing toolbar.

*Note: If ⬛ is not displayed,
click ⁇ on the Standard toolbar
to display all the buttons.*

3 Click ⬝ in this area
to select a color.

4 Click the color you
want to use.

■ The graphic displays
the new color.

*Note: To hide the Drawing
toolbar, repeat step 2.*

■ To remove the color
from a graphic, repeat
steps 1 to 4, except
select **No Fill** in step 4.

MAKE A GRAPHIC 3-D

You can make a graphic in your worksheet or chart appear three-dimensional.

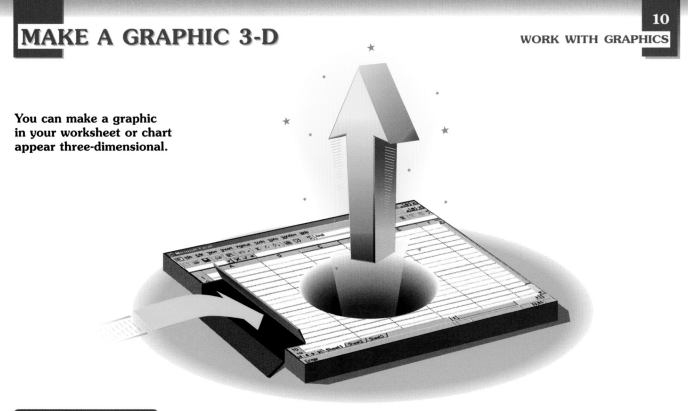

MAKE A GRAPHIC 3-D

1 Click the graphic you want to appear three-dimensional.

2 Click 🖳 to display the Drawing toolbar.

Note: If 🖳 is not displayed, click 🔽 on the Standard toolbar to display all the buttons.

3 Click 🔲 to select a 3-D effect.

4 Click the 3-D effect you want to use.

Note: If the 3-D effects are dimmed, you cannot make the graphic you selected three-dimensional.

■ The graphic displays the 3-D effect.

Note: To hide the Drawing toolbar, repeat step 2.

■ To remove a 3-D effect from a graphic, repeat steps **1** to **4**, except select **No 3-D** in step **4**.

ROTATE A GRAPHIC

You can rotate
a graphic in
your worksheet.

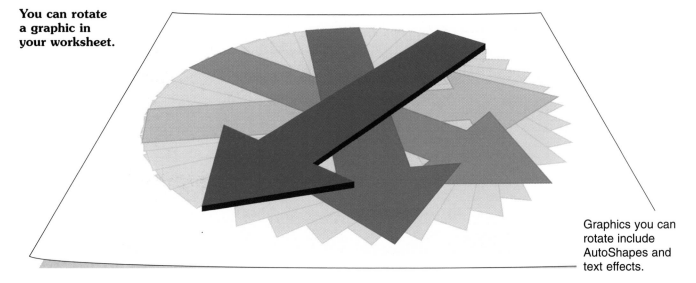

Graphics you can
rotate include
AutoShapes and
text effects.

ROTATE A GRAPHIC

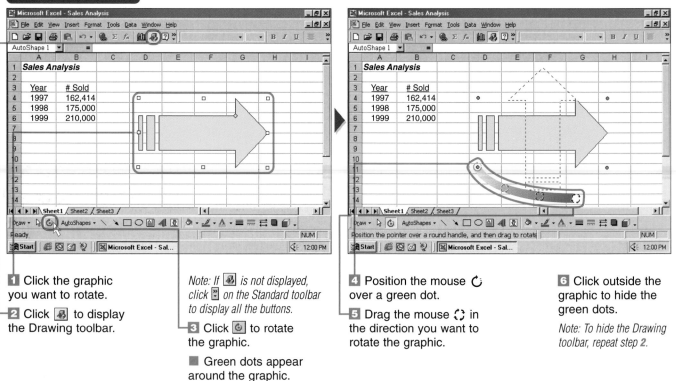

1 Click the graphic
you want to rotate.

2 Click 🖼 to display
the Drawing toolbar.

*Note: If 🖼 is not displayed,
click ⏵ on the Standard toolbar
to display all the buttons.*

3 Click 🔄 to rotate
the graphic.

■ Green dots appear
around the graphic.

4 Position the mouse ↻
over a green dot.

5 Drag the mouse ✧ in
the direction you want to
rotate the graphic.

6 Click outside the
graphic to hide the
green dots.

*Note: To hide the Drawing
toolbar, repeat step 2.*

You can add a shadow to add depth to a graphic in your worksheet.

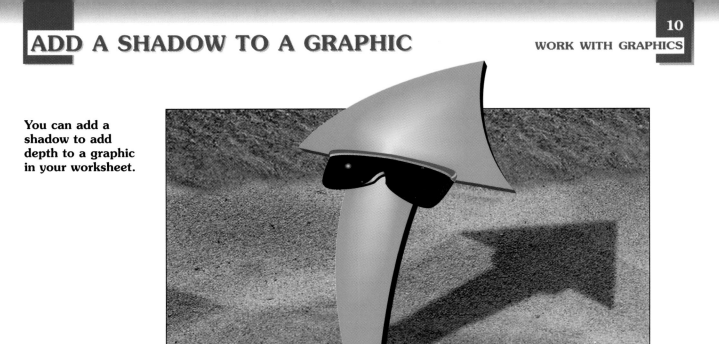

ADD A SHADOW TO A GRAPHIC

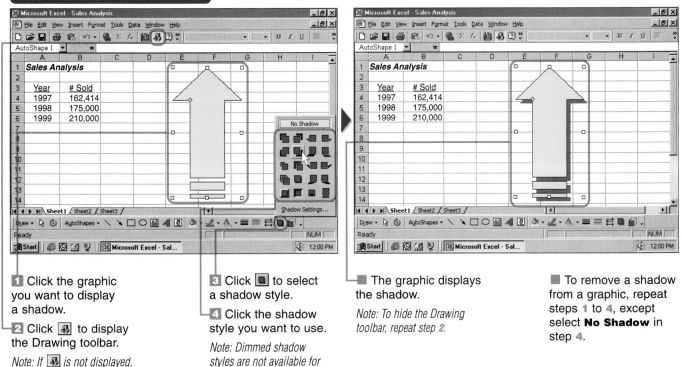

1 Click the graphic you want to display a shadow.

2 Click 🔲 to display the Drawing toolbar.

Note: If 🔲 is not displayed, click 🔲 on the Standard toolbar to display all the buttons.

3 Click 🔲 to select a shadow style.

4 Click the shadow style you want to use.

Note: Dimmed shadow styles are not available for the graphic you selected.

■ The graphic displays the shadow.

Note: To hide the Drawing toolbar, repeat step 2.

■ To remove a shadow from a graphic, repeat steps **1** to **4**, except select **No Shadow** in step **4**.

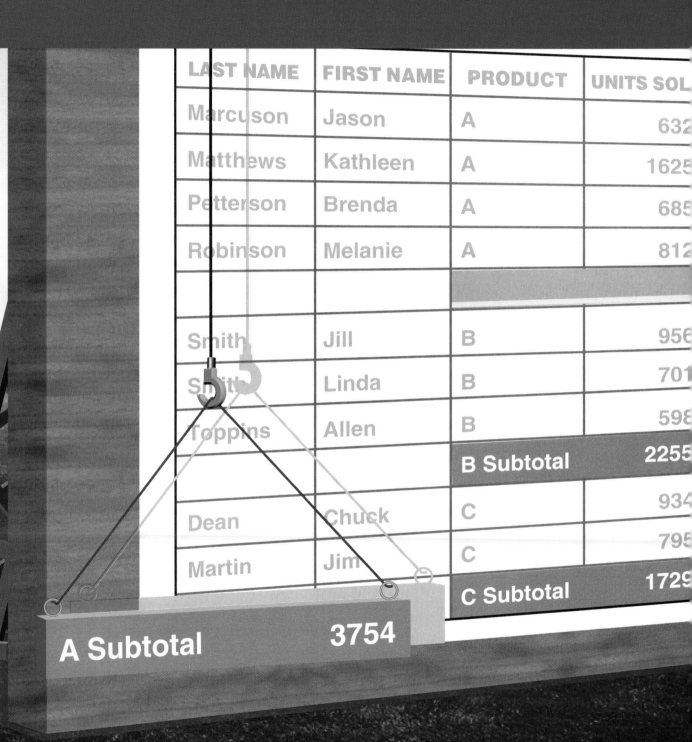

LAST NAME	FIRST NAME	PRODUCT	UNITS SOL
Marcuson	Jason	A	632
Matthews	Kathleen	A	1625
Petterson	Brenda	A	685
Robinson	Melanie	A	812
A Subtotal			**3754**
Smith	Jill	B	956
Smith	Linda	B	701
Toppins	Allen	B	598
B Subtotal			**2255**
Dean	Chuck	C	934
Martin	Jim	C	795
C Subtotal			**1729**

CHAPTER 11

Manage Data in a List

Would you like Excel to help you organize a large collection of data? In this chapter you will learn how to sort data in a list, add subtotals to a list and more.

CREATE A LIST

You can create a list to organize a large collection of data.

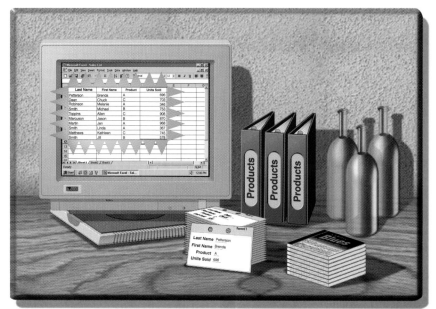

Common lists include mailing lists, phone directories, product lists, library book catalogs, music collections and wine lists.

CREATE A LIST

1 Type the column labels that describe the data you will enter into each column.

Note: You should bold the column labels to ensure that Excel will recognize the text as column labels. To bold text, see page 132.

2 Type the information for each record. Do not leave any blank rows in the list.

ADD RECORDS USING A DATA FORM

1 Click a cell in the list.

2 Click **Data**.

3 Click **Form**.

Note: If Form does not appear on the menu, position the mouse ⟍ over the bottom of the menu to display all the menu commands.

What are column labels and records?

Last Name	First Name	Product	Units Sold
Petterson	Brenda	A	696
Dean	Chuck	C	703
Robinson	Melanie	A	346
Smith	Michael	B	753
Toppins	Allen	C	908
Marcuson	Jason	B	870
Martin	Jen	A	968
Smith	Linda	A	367
Matthews	Kathleen	C	745
Smith	Jill	B	578

Column Labels

A column label describes the data in a column. The first row in a list contains the column labels for the list.

Records

A record is a group of related data. Each row in a list contains one record.

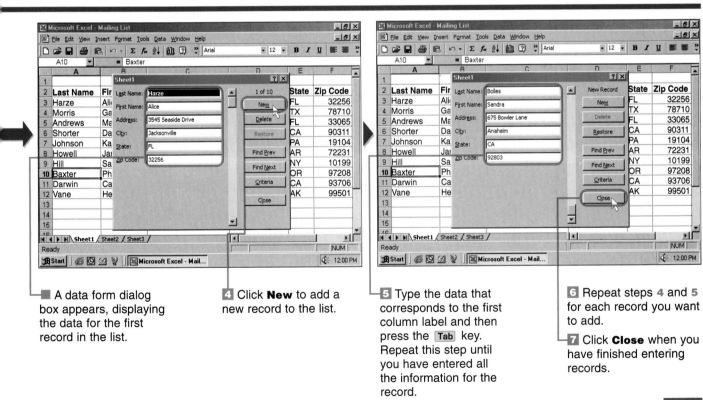

■ A data form dialog box appears, displaying the data for the first record in the list.

4 Click **New** to add a new record to the list.

5 Type the data that corresponds to the first column label and then press the Tab key. Repeat this step until you have entered all the information for the record.

6 Repeat steps 4 and 5 for each record you want to add.

7 Click **Close** when you have finished entering records.

EDIT DATA IN A LIST

You can edit data in a list to update the data or correct a mistake. You can also delete a record to remove data you no longer need from the list.

Sheet1

Last Name:	Hill
First Name:	~~Susan~~ *Sarah*
Address:	689 Explorer Road
City:	New ~~York~~ *York*
State:	NY
Zip Code:	10199

EDIT DATA IN A LIST

1 Click a cell in the list.

2 Click **Data**.

3 Click **Form**.

Note: If Form does not appear on the menu, position the mouse over the bottom of the menu to display all the menu commands.

■ A data form dialog box appears, displaying the data for the first record in the list.

4 Click one of the following options to browse through the records.

Find Prev - Display previous record

Find Next - Display next record

■ This area shows the number of the displayed record and the total number of records in the list.

Note: You can also use the scroll bar to browse through the records.

?

Can I make changes to my list directly in the worksheet?

You can edit data directly in the worksheet to update or correct the data in your list. To edit data in a worksheet, see page 50.

You can also delete a row to remove a record you no longer need from your list. To delete a row, see page 72.

DELETE A RECORD

5 Repeat step **4** until the record you want to edit appears.

6 Double-click the data you want to change and then type the new data.

■ To immediately cancel a change you made to a record, click **Restore**.

7 When you finish editing the data, click **Close** to close the data form dialog box.

1 Perform steps **1** to **4** on page 252 to display the record you want to delete in the data form dialog box.

2 Click **Delete**.

■ A dialog box appears, confirming the deletion.

3 Click **OK** to permanently delete the record.

4 Click **Close** to close the data form dialog box.

FIND DATA IN A LIST

You can search
for records that
contain specific
data in your list.

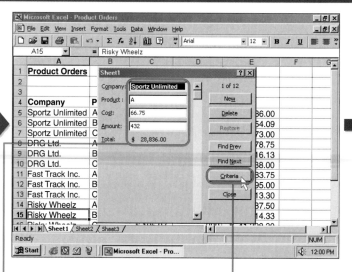

For example, you can
have Excel find all the
records for clients who
live in California.

FIND DATA IN A LIST

1 Click a cell in
the list.

2 Click **Data**.

3 Click **Form**.

*Note: If Form does not appear
on the menu, position the
mouse ⌖ over the bottom
of the menu to display all
the menu commands.*

■ A data form dialog
box appears, displaying
the data for the first
record in the list.

4 Click **Criteria** to
specify the data you
want to search for.

**What operators can I use to search
for specific data in my list?**

Operator	Example	Result
=	=100	Finds data equal to 100
>	>100	Finds data greater than 100
<	<100	Finds data less than 100
>=	>=100	Finds data greater than or equal to 100
<=	<=100	Finds data less than or equal to 100
<>	<>100	Finds data not equal to 100

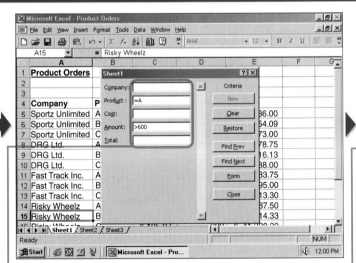

5 Click the area
beside the label of
the column you want
to use to find data.

6 Type an operator
for the search and
then type the data
you want to find.

*Note: For information on operators,
see the top of this page.*

■ You can use more than
one column to search for
data. For example, you can
find all the companies that
bought more than 600 units
of product A.

7 Click one of the
following options.

Find Prev - Display
previous matching
record

Find Next - Display
next matching record

8 Repeat step **7** until
you finish viewing all
the matching records.

9 Click **Close** to close
the data form dialog box.

SORT DATA IN A LIST

You can organize your
list by changing the
order of the data.

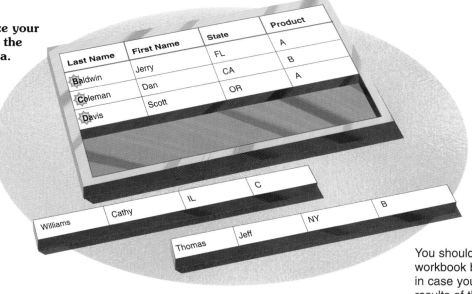

You should save your
workbook before sorting data
in case you do not like the
results of the sort. To save
a workbook, see page 28.

SORT BY ONE COLUMN

1 Click a cell in the
column you want to
sort by.

2 Click the way you
want to sort the data.

$\boxed{A\downarrow}$ Sort 0 to 9, A to Z

$\boxed{Z\downarrow}$ Sort 9 to 0, Z to A

*Note: If the button you want
is not displayed, click* $\boxed{»}$
*on the Standard toolbar
to display all the buttons.*

■ The data in the
list appears in the
new order.

■ In this example,
the data is sorted
by last name.

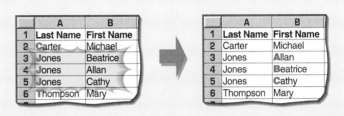

?

Why would I sort my data by more than one column?

Sorting by more than one column allows you to further organize the data in your list. For example, if a last name appears more than once in the Last Name column, you can sort by a second column, such as the First Name column.

SORT BY TWO COLUMNS

1 Click a cell in the list.

2 Click **Data**.

3 Click **Sort**.

■ The Sort dialog box appears.

4 Click ▼ in this area to select the first column you want to sort by.

5 Click the name of the first column you want to sort by.

CONTINUED ▶

SORT DATA IN A LIST

You can sort the data in your list by letter, number or date.

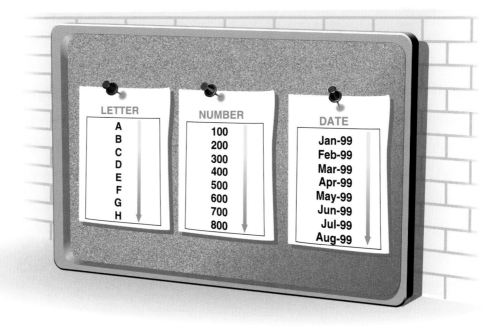

LETTER	NUMBER	DATE
A	100	Jan-99
B	200	Feb-99
C	300	Mar-99
D	400	Apr-99
E	500	May-99
F	600	Jun-99
G	700	Jul-99
H	800	Aug-99

SORT BY TWO COLUMNS (CONTINUED)

6 Click the way you want to sort the first column (○ changes to ⊙).

Ascending
Sort 0 to 9, A to Z

Descending
Sort 9 to 0, Z to A

7 Click ▼ in this area to select the second column you want to sort by.

8 Click the name of the column you want to sort by.

How often can I sort the data in my list?

You can sort the data in your list as often as you like. Sorting is useful if you frequently add new data to your list.

▤ Click the way you want to sort the second column (○ changes to ⊙).

⤒ Click **OK** to sort the data.

■ The data in the list appears in the new order.

■ In this example, the data is sorted by state. When a state appears more than once in the list, the data is then sorted by city.

FILTER A LIST

You can filter your list to display only the records containing the data you want to review.

The AutoFilter feature allows you to analyze your data by placing related records together and hiding the records you do not want to review.

FILTER A LIST

1 Click a cell in the list.

2 Click **Data**.

3 Click **Filter**.

4 Click **AutoFilter**.

■ An arrow (▼) appears beside each column label.

5 Click ▼ in the column containing the data you want to use to filter the list.

6 Click the data you want to use to filter the list.

260

How do I turn off the AutoFilter feature when I no longer want to filter my list?

To turn off the AutoFilter feature, repeat steps **2** to **4** on page 260.

■ The list displays only the records containing the data you specified. The other records are temporarily hidden.

■ In this example, the list displays only the records for players who have played 58 games.

REDISPLAY ALL RECORDS

1 To once again display all the records, click ▼ in the column containing the data you used to filter the list.

2 Click **(All)**.

FILTER A LIST

You can filter your list
to display only records
containing data within
a specific range.

For example, you can
display records for
employees whose
sales are greater than
or equal to $500.

FILTER A LIST BY COMPARING DATA

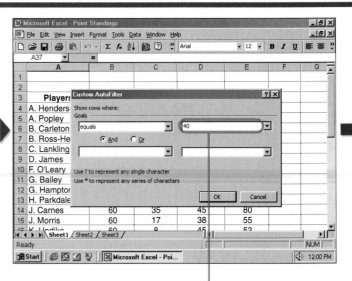

1 To turn on the AutoFilter
feature, perform steps **1**
to **4** on page 260.

■ An arrow (▼) appears
beside each column label.

2 Click ▼ in the
column containing the
data you want to use
to filter the list.

3 Click **(Custom...)**.

■ The Custom AutoFilter
dialog box appears.

4 Type the data you
want Excel to compare
to each record in the list.

How can I compare data in my list?

Excel offers many ways you can compare data to help you analyze the data in your list.

equals
does not equal
is greater than
is greater than or equal to
is less than
is less than or equal to
begins with
does not begin with
ends with
does not end with
contains
does not contain

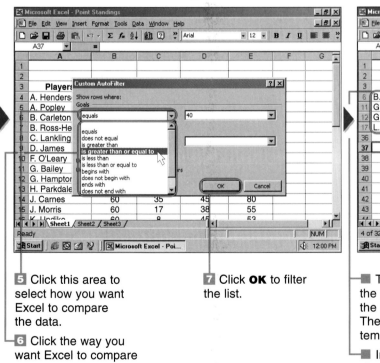

5 Click this area to select how you want Excel to compare the data.

6 Click the way you want Excel to compare the data.

7 Click **OK** to filter the list.

■ The list displays only the records containing the data you specified. The other records are temporarily hidden.

■ In this example, the list displays only the records for players who have scored 40 goals or more.

■ To once again display all the records, perform steps **1** and **2** on page 261.

■ To turn off the AutoFilter feature, perform steps **2** to **4** on page 260.

ADD SUBTOTALS TO A LIST

You can quickly summarize data by adding subtotals to your list.

Last Name	First Name	Product	Units Sold
Marcuson	Jason	A	632
Mathews	Kathleen	A	1625
Petterson	Brenda	A	685
Robinson	Melanie	A	812
		A Total	3754
Smith	Jill	B	956
Smith	Linda	B	701
Toppins	Allen	B	598
		B Total	2255
Dean	Chuck	C	934
Martin	Jim	C	795
		C Total	1729

ADD SUBTOTALS TO A LIST

1 Sort the column you want to display subtotals for. To sort data, see page 256.

Note: In this example, the Product column is sorted.

2 Click a cell in the list.

3 Click **Data**.

4 Click **Subtotals**.

■ The Subtotal dialog box appears.

5 Click this area to select the column you want to display subtotals for.

6 Click the name of the column you want to display subtotals for.

Note: The column you select should be the same column you sorted in step 1.

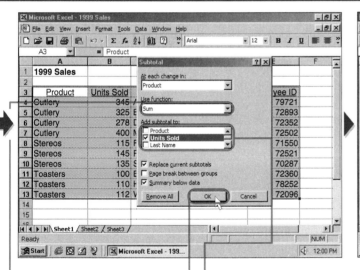

How can subtotals help me?

You can use subtotals to help you analyze the data in your list and create a report for the data. For example, in a list containing department names and sales figures, you can use subtotals to find the total sales for each department and the grand total of all the sales.

QUARTERLY REPORT

Department	Salesperson	Sales
Automotive	L. Smith	$5,900
Automotive	M. Johnson	$8,500
Automotive	L. Hearn	$5,500
Automotive Total		**$19,900**
Housewares	C. Dean	$10,850
Housewares	G. Church	$4,000
Housewares	J. Smith	$5,000
Housewares Total		**$19,850**
Sports	J. Martin	$8,800
Sports	K. Gan	$10,000
Sports	J. Gledhill	$5,500
Sports Total		**$24,300**
Grand Total		**$64,050**

■ This area displays the calculation Excel will perform. You can click this area to select a different calculation.

■ This area displays a check mark (☑) beside each column Excel will subtotal. You can click the box beside a column to add (☑) or remove (☐) a check mark.

7 Click **OK** to add the subtotals to the list.

■ The list displays the subtotals and a grand total.

ADD SUBTOTALS TO A LIST

After adding subtotals to your list, you can display just the grand total, the subtotals or all the data in the list.

| GRAND TOTAL | SUBTOTALS | ALL THE DATA |

GRAND TOTAL

Last Name	First Name	Product	Units Sold
		Grand Total	8316

SUBTOTALS

Last Name	First Name	Product	Units Sold
		A Total	3754
		B Total	2255
		C Total	2307
		Grand Total	8316

ALL THE DATA

Last Name	First Name	Product	Units Sold
Marcuson	Jason	A	632
Matthews	Kathleen	A	1625
Petterson	Brenda	A	685
Robinson	Melanie	A	812
		A Total	3754
Smith	Jill	B	956
Smith	Linda	B	701
Toppins	Allen	B	598
		B Total	2255
Dean	Chuck	C	934
Martin	Jim	C	795
Smith	Michael	C	578
		C Total	2307
		Grand Total	8316

HIDE OR DISPLAY SUBTOTALED DATA

	A	B	C	D	E
3	Product	Units Sold	Last Name	First Name	Employee ID
4	Cutlery	345	Anderson	Angela	79721
5	Cutlery	325	Bernhart	Sara	72893
6	Cutlery	278	Devison	Paul	72352
7	Cutlery	400	Mills	Michael	72502
8	**Cutlery Total**	1348			
9	Stereos	115	Fisher	Kim	71550
10	Stereos	145	Roberts	Greg	72521
11	Stereos	135	Sanderson	Roger	70287
12	**Stereos Total**	395			
13	Toasters	100	Blackburn	Laurie	72360
14	Toasters	110	Harris	Mindy	78252
15	Toasters	112	Wilson	Ken	72096
16	**Toasters Total**	322			
17	**Grand Total**	2065			

	A	B	C	D	E
3	Product	Units Sold	Last Name	First Name	Employee ID
8	**Cutlery Total**	1348			
12	**Stereos Total**	395			
16	**Toasters Total**	322			
17	**Grand Total**	2065			

■1 Click one of these buttons.

1 Display only grand total

2 Display subtotals and grand total

3 Display all the data

■ Excel displays the data you specified. The other data is temporarily hidden.

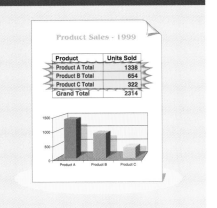

?

Can I create a chart based on the subtotals in my list?

Yes. Perform step **1** on page 266, selecting **2** to display the subtotals and grand total in the list. You can then create a chart to graphically illustrate the subtotals. To create a chart, see page 208.

REMOVE SUBTOTALS

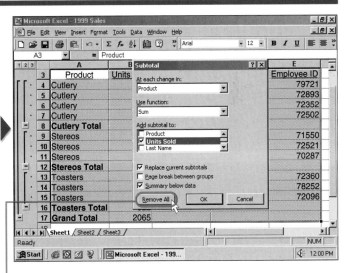

1 Click a cell in the list.

2 Click **Data**.

3 Click **Subtotals**.

■ The Subtotal dialog box appears.

4 Click **Remove All** to remove the subtotals from the list.

CHAPTER 12

Time-Saving Features

Would you like to learn how to customize Excel to help you save time? In this chapter you will learn how to create your own toolbars, speed up tasks using macros and much more.

EMPLOYEE	HOURS
Ken Thompson	44
Mary Bennet	38
George Costello	52
Kimberly Fisher	37.5
Paul Duncan	37
Shirley Allison	40
Brian Williams	50
	53.5
	41

ours for Apr. 12-16

5-9

CREATE A CUSTOM SERIES

You can create a series of text or numbers that you can quickly enter into your worksheets. This is useful if you frequently enter the same data, such as a list of employee names or product numbers.

CREATE A CUSTOM SERIES

1 Type the text or numbers you want to save as a series.

Note: To include numbers in the series, you must type an apostrophe (') in front of each number.

2 Select the cells containing the text or numbers you entered. To select cells, see page 16.

3 Click **Tools**.

4 Click **Options**.

■ The Options dialog box appears.

270

How do I use the custom series I created?

To use a series you created, perform steps 1 to 4 on page 18. If the first item in your series is a number, you must type an apostrophe (') in front of the number when you use the series.

Product #
'957432
564830
176948

5 Click the **Custom Lists** tab.

6 Click **Import** to create the custom series.

■ This area displays the text or numbers in the series.

7 Click **OK** to confirm your change.

CREATE A NEW TOOLBAR

You can create a new
toolbar containing
buttons and commands
you frequently use.

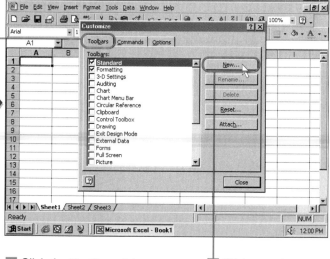

Creating a toolbar allows
you to have a specific
toolbar for each type
of task you regularly
perform, such as printing
workbooks or adding
AutoShapes.

CREATE A NEW TOOLBAR

■1 Click **Tools**.

■2 Click **Customize**.

■ The Customize dialog
box appears.

■3 Click the **Toolbars** tab.

■4 Click **New** to create
a new toolbar.

■ The New Toolbar
dialog box appears.

How can I move a toolbar I created?

After you create a new toolbar, you can move the toolbar to a new location on your screen. To move a toolbar, position the mouse ▷ over the title bar and then drag the toolbar to a new location. For more information on working with toolbars, see pages 118 to 121.

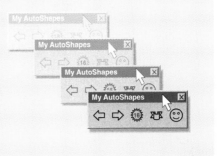

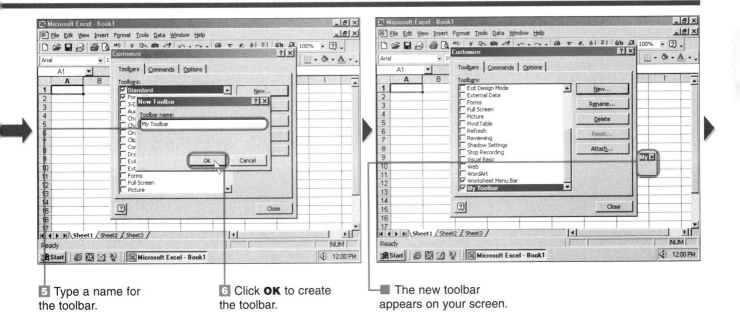

5 Type a name for the toolbar.

6 Click **OK** to create the toolbar.

■ The new toolbar appears on your screen.

CONTINUED

CREATE A NEW TOOLBAR

You can add buttons to
a toolbar you created.
Each button allows you
to perform a different
task.

Excel offers hundreds
of buttons for you to
choose from.

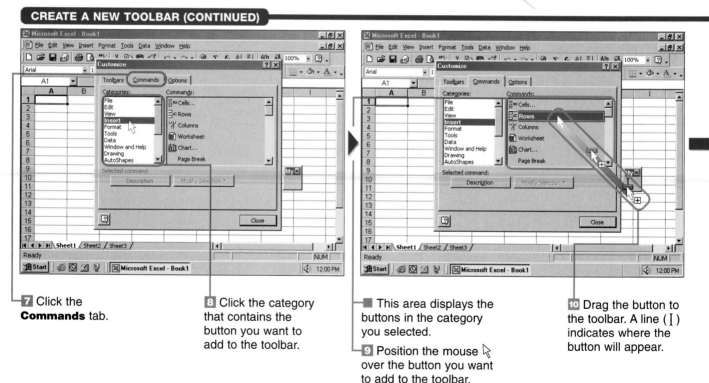

7 Click the
Commands tab.

8 Click the category
that contains the
button you want to
add to the toolbar.

■ This area displays the
buttons in the category
you selected.

9 Position the mouse
over the button you want
to add to the toolbar.

10 Drag the button to
the toolbar. A line ([ )
indicates where the
button will appear.

Can I add a button to a toolbar included with Excel?

Yes. Display the Customize dialog box by performing steps 1 and 2 on page 272. Then perform steps 7 to 12 below to add a button to the toolbar.

STANDARD TOOLBAR

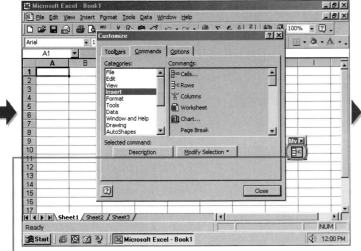

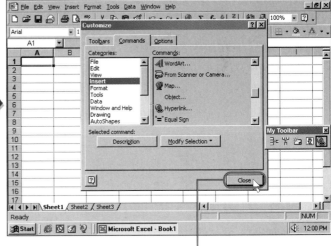

■ The button appears on the toolbar.

■11■ Repeat steps 8 to 10 for each button you want to add to the toolbar.

■12■ When you finish adding buttons to the toolbar, click **Close** to close the Customize dialog box.

CREATE A NEW TOOLBAR

You can move buttons on your toolbar to place buttons for related tasks together. This can make it easier to find the buttons you need.

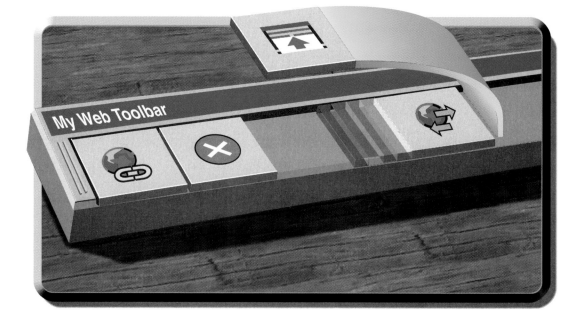

MOVE A BUTTON

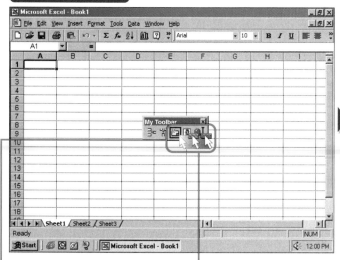

1 Display the toolbar you want to change. To display a toolbar, see page 118.

2 Position the mouse ⟍ over the button you want to move.

3 Press and hold down the Alt key as you drag the button to a new location.

■ A line (I) indicates where the button will appear.

■ The button appears in the new location on the toolbar.

You can remove buttons you no longer use from your toolbar.

REMOVE A BUTTON

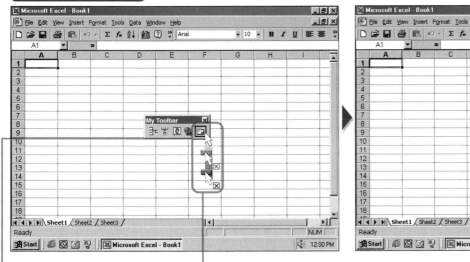

1 Display the toolbar you want to change. To display a toolbar, see page 118.

2 Position the mouse over the button you want to remove.

3 Press and hold down the Alt key as you drag the button downward off the toolbar.

■ The button disappears from the toolbar.

RECORD A MACRO

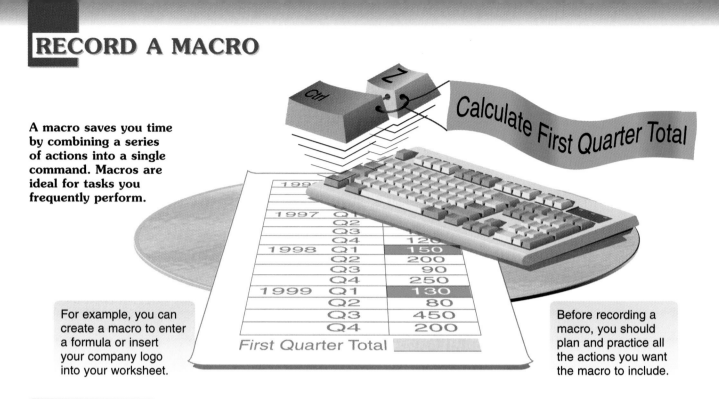

A macro saves you time by combining a series of actions into a single command. Macros are ideal for tasks you frequently perform.

For example, you can create a macro to enter a formula or insert your company logo into your worksheet.

Before recording a macro, you should plan and practice all the actions you want the macro to include.

Calculate First Quarter Total

199_		
1997	Q2	
	Q3	
	Q4	120
1998	Q1	150
	Q2	200
	Q3	90
	Q4	250
1999	Q1	130
	Q2	80
	Q3	450
	Q4	200

First Quarter Total

RECORD A MACRO

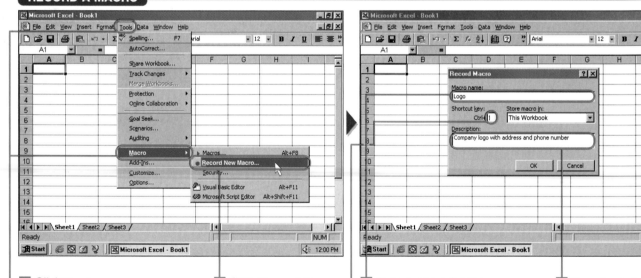

1 Click **Tools**.

2 Click **Macro**.

Note: If Macro does not appear on the menu, position the mouse over the bottom of the menu to display all the menu commands.

3 Click **Record New Macro**.

■ The Record Macro dialog box appears.

4 Type a name for the macro. The name must begin with a letter and cannot contain spaces.

5 To assign a keyboard shortcut to the macro, click this area. Then type the letter you want to use with the **Ctrl** key as the shortcut.

6 To enter a description for the macro, drag the mouse I over the text in this area to highlight the text. Then type a description.

Where can I store a macro?

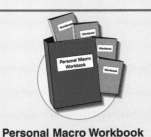

Personal Macro Workbook

If you want to use a macro with all your workbooks, you can store the macro in the Personal Macro Workbook.

New Workbook

You can have Excel create a new workbook to store the macro. You will only be able to use the macro when the new workbook is open.

This Workbook

You can store the macro in the current workbook. You will only be able to use the macro when this workbook is open.

7 Click this area to specify the location where you want Excel to store the macro.

8 Click the location where you want to store the macro.

9 Click **OK** to continue.

■ The Stop Recording toolbar appears.

10 If you want to be able to run the macro in any cell in a worksheet, click 🖾 .

11 Perform the actions you want the macro to include.

12 Click ■ when you have completed all the actions you want the macro to include.

Note: To run a macro, see page 280.

RUN A MACRO

When you run a macro, Excel automatically performs the actions you recorded.

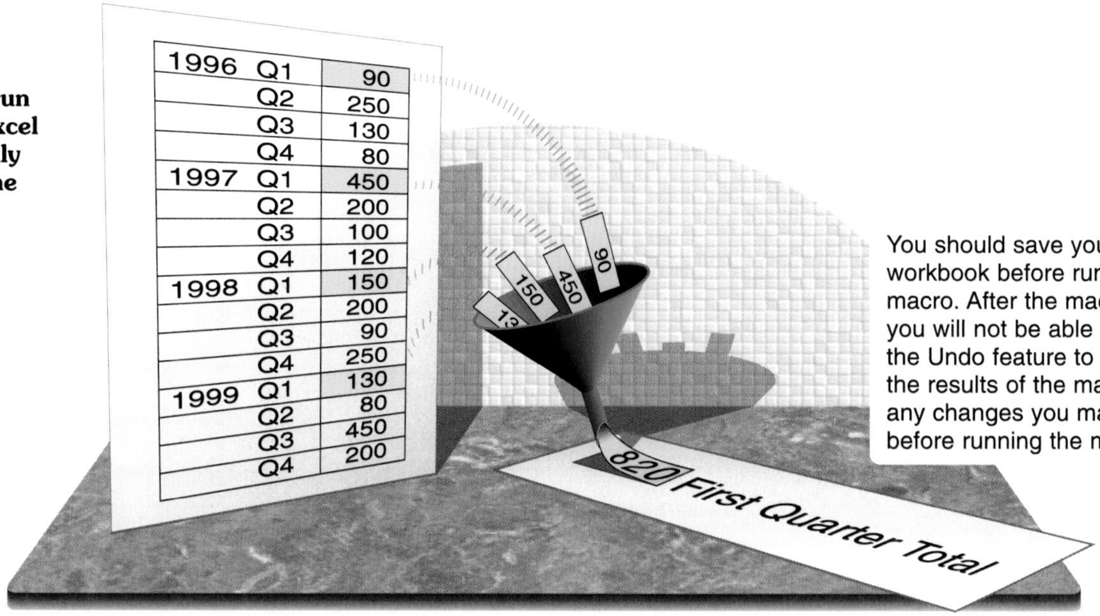

1996 Q1 90
Q2 250
Q3 130
Q4 80
1997 Q1 450
Q2 200
Q3 100
Q4 120
1998 Q1 150
Q2 200
Q3 90
Q4 250
1999 Q1 130
Q2 80
Q3 450
Q4 200
820 First Quarter Total

You should save your workbook before running a macro. After the macro runs, you will not be able to use the Undo feature to reverse the results of the macro or any changes you made before running the macro.

RUN A MACRO

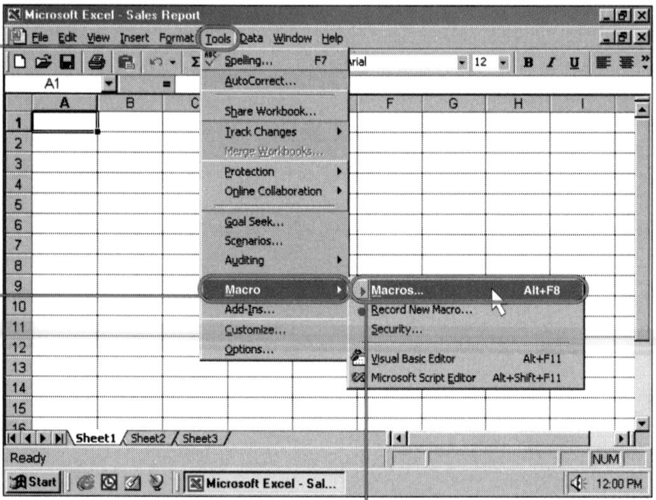

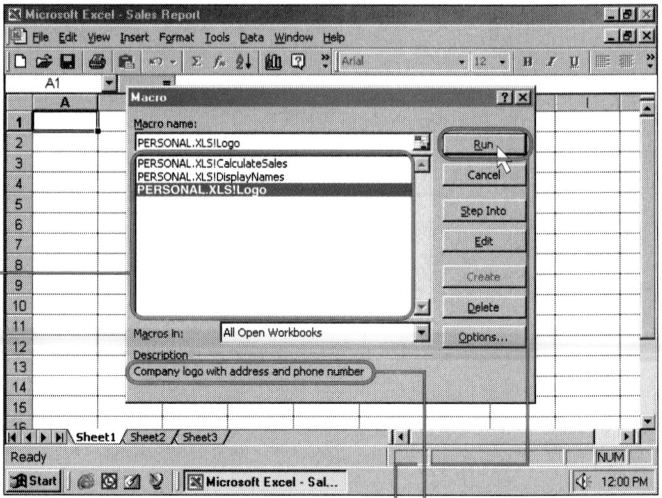

1 If you want the macro to affect specific cells in your worksheet, select the cells you want to change. To select cells, see page 16.

2 Click **Tools**.

3 Click **Macro**.

Note: If Macro does not appear on the menu, position the mouse over the bottom of the menu to display all the menu commands.

4 Click **Macros**.

■ The Macro dialog box appears.

■ This area lists the available macros. Macros you stored in the Personal Macro Workbook begin with PERSONAL.XLS!.

5 Click the name of the macro you want to run.

■ This area displays the description of the macro you selected.

6 Click **Run** to run the macro.

Why does a warning dialog box appear when I open a workbook containing a macro?

Some macros may contain viruses that could damage your computer.

> **Microsoft Excel** ? X
>
> C:\My Documents\Sales Analysis.xls contains macros.
>
> Macros may contain viruses. It is always safe to disable macros, but if the macros are legitimate, you might lose some functionality.
>
> [Disable Macros]   [Enable Macros]   [More Info]

■ If the workbook is not from a trusted source, click **Disable Macros** to open the workbook without the macros.

■ If the workbook is from a trusted source, click **Enable Macros** to open the workbook.

■ The macro performs the actions you recorded.

■ In this example, the macro entered the company information into the worksheet.

RUN A MACRO USING THE KEYBOARD

1 If you want the macro to affect specific cells in your worksheet, select the cells you want to change. To select cells, see page 16.

2 Press the keyboard shortcut you assigned to the macro.

■ The macro performs the actions you recorded.

CHAPTER 13

Excel and the Internet

Are you wondering how you can use Excel to share data with other people on the Internet? In this chapter you will learn how to e-mail a worksheet, save a workbook as a Web page and more.

Sportz Inc.
UNIT SALES BY STATE

Colorado	
Florida	89,000
Maine	59,000
Ohio	52,000
Utah	43,00

E-MAIL A WORKSHEET

You can e-mail the worksheet displayed on your screen to a friend, family member or colleague.

Before you can e-mail a worksheet, Microsoft Outlook must be set up on your computer. Microsoft Outlook is a program that allows you to send and receive e-mail messages.

E-MAIL A WORKSHEET

1 Click 📧 to e-mail the current worksheet.

Note: If 📧 is not displayed, click 🔽 on the Standard toolbar to display all the buttons.

■ If the workbook contains data in more than one worksheet, a message appears, asking if you want to send the entire workbook or just the current worksheet.

2 Click this option to send the current worksheet.

■ An area appears for you to address the message.

3 Click this area and type the e-mail address of each person you want to receive the message. Separate each address with a semicolon (;).

?

How do I e-mail an entire workbook?

To e-mail an entire workbook, perform steps **1** to **5** below, except select **Send the entire workbook as an attachment** in step **2**. Then click **Send** to send the message.

When you e-mail an entire workbook, the workbook appears as an icon in the message.

4 To send a copy of the message, click this area and type the e-mail address of each person you want to receive a copy. Separate each address with a semicolon (;).

Note: You may want to send a copy of the message to people who are not directly involved but would be interested in the message.

5 Click this area and type a subject for the message.

Note: If a subject already exists, you can drag the mouse I over the existing subject and then type a new subject.

6 Click **Send this Sheet** to send the message.

CREATE A HYPERLINK

You can create a hyperlink to connect data in your workbook to another document on your computer, network, corporate intranet or the Internet.

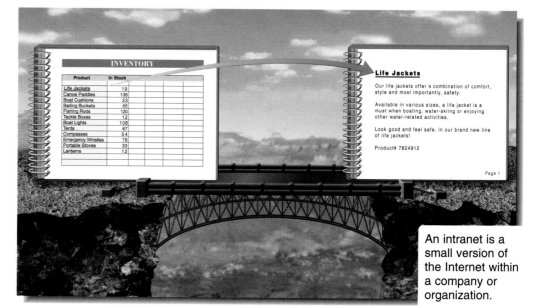

An intranet is a small version of the Internet within a company or organization.

CREATE A HYPERLINK

1 Select the cells containing the data you want to make a hyperlink. To select cells, see page 16.

2 Click 🐘 to create a hyperlink.

Note: If 🐘 is not displayed, click ▸ on the Standard toolbar to display all the buttons.

■ The Insert Hyperlink dialog box appears.

Can I make a graphic a hyperlink?

Yes. If your workbook contains a graphic, such as an AutoShape or text effect, you can make the graphic a hyperlink. To make a graphic a hyperlink, click the graphic and then perform steps 2 to 7, starting on page 286.

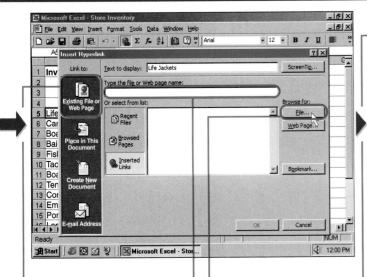

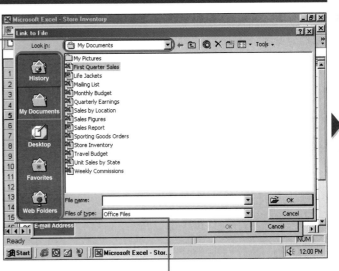

■3 Click **Existing File or Web Page** to link the data to an existing document.

■4 To link the data to a document on your computer or network, click **File**.

■ To link the data to a page on the Web, click this area and then type the address of the Web page (example: www.maran.com). Then skip to step 7 on page 288.

■ The Link to File dialog box appears.

■ This area shows the location of the displayed documents. You can click this area to change the location.

■ This area allows you to access commonly used folders. To display the contents of a folder, click the folder.

Note: For information on the commonly used folders, see the top of page 29.

CONTINUED ▶

CREATE A HYPERLINK

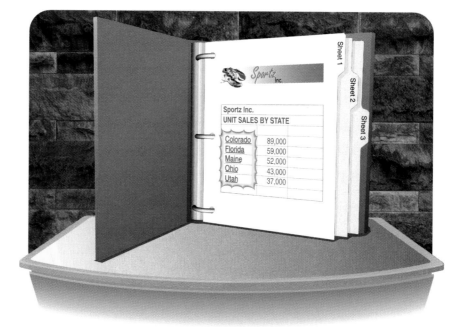

You can easily identify hyperlinks in your workbook. Hyperlinks appear underlined and in color.

CREATE A HYPERLINK (CONTINUED)

-5 Click the name of the document you want to link the data to.

-6 Click **OK** to confirm your selection.

-■ This area displays the address of the document you selected.

-7 Click **OK** to create the hyperlink.

? Can Excel automatically create a hyperlink for me?

When you type the address of a document located on your network or the Internet, Excel will automatically change the address to a hyperlink for you.

■ Excel creates the hyperlink. Hyperlinks appear underlined and in color.

■ When you position the mouse 🖑 over the hyperlink, a yellow box appears, displaying where the hyperlink will take you.

SELECT A HYPERLINK

1 Click a hyperlink to display the document or Web page connected to the hyperlink.

■ The document or Web page connected to the hyperlink appears.

■ If the hyperlink connects to a Web page, your Web browser will open and display the page.

2 When you finish reviewing the document or Web page, click ⊠ to close the window.

PREVIEW A WORKBOOK AS A WEB PAGE

You can preview how your workbook will look as a Web page. This allows you to see how the workbook will appear on the Internet or your company's intranet.

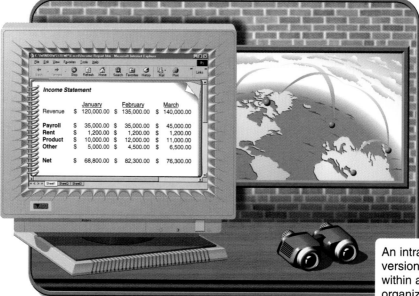

An intranet is a small version of the Internet within a company or organization.

PREVIEW A WORKBOOK AS A WEB PAGE

1 Open the workbook you want to preview as a Web page. To open a workbook, see page 38.

2 Click **File**.

3 Click **Web Page Preview** to preview your workbook as a Web page.

Will my Web page look the same to everyone who views the Web page?

No. Different Web browsers may display your Web page differently. Many Web browsers are used on the Web. The two most popular Web browsers are Microsoft Internet Explorer and Netscape Navigator.

Microsoft Internet Explorer

Netscape Navigator

■ Your Web browser window opens, displaying your workbook as a Web page.

■ 4 To maximize the Web browser window to fill your screen, click 🗖.

■ The gridlines that separate each cell do not appear in the Web browser window.

■ If your workbook contains more than one worksheet, this area displays a tab for each worksheet.

■ 5 To display the contents of a different worksheet, click a tab.

6 When you finish reviewing your workbook as a Web page, click ⊠ to close the Web browser window.

SAVE A WORKBOOK AS A WEB PAGE

You can save a
workbook as a Web
page. This lets you
place the workbook
on the Internet or
your company's
intranet.

An intranet is a small
version of the Internet
within a company or
organization.

SAVE A WORKBOOK AS A WEB PAGE

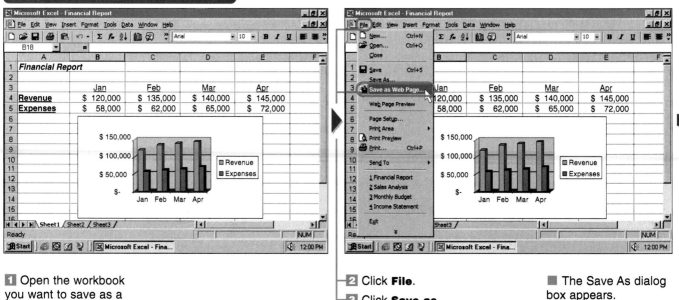

1 Open the workbook
you want to save as a
Web page. To open a
workbook, see page 38.

2 Click **File**.

3 Click **Save as
Web Page**.

■ The Save As dialog
box appears.

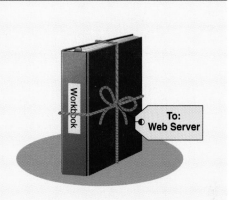

How do I make my Web page available for other people to view?

After you save your workbook as a Web page, you can transfer the page to a computer that stores Web pages, called a Web server. Once you publish the Web page on a Web server, the page will be available for other people to view. For more information on publishing a Web page, contact your network administrator or Internet service provider.

■4 Type a file name for the Web page.

■ This area shows the location where Excel will store the Web page. You can click this area to change the location.

■ This area allows you to access commonly used folders. To display the contents of a folder, click the folder.

Note: For information on the commonly used folders, see the top of page 29.

■5 Click an option to specify whether you want to save the entire workbook or just the current worksheet as a Web page (○ changes to ⊙).

■6 Click **Save** to save the Web page.

INDEX

INDEX

INDEX

INDEX

INDEX

X

Z

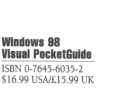

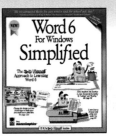

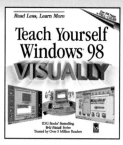

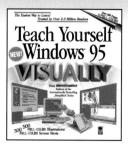
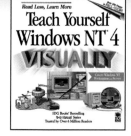

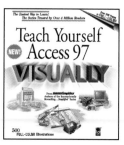

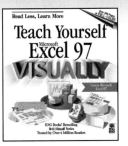

TRADE & INDIVIDUAL ORDERS

Phone: **(800) 762-2974**
or **(317) 596-5200**
(8 a.m. – 6 p.m., CST, weekdays)
FAX : **(800) 550-2747**
or **(317) 596-5692**

EDUCATIONAL ORDERS & DISCOUNTS

Phone: **(800) 434-2086**
(8:30 a.m.–5:00 p.m., CST, weekdays)
FAX : **(317) 596-5499**

CORPORATE ORDERS FOR 3-D VISUAL™ SERIES

Phone: **(800) 469-6616**
(8 a.m.–5 p.m., EST, weekdays)
FAX : **(905) 890-9434**

Qty	ISBN	Title	Price	Total

Shipping & Handling Charges

	Description	First book	Each add'l. book	Total
Domestic	Normal	$4.50	$1.50	$
	Two Day Air	$8.50	$2.50	$
	Overnight	$18.00	$3.00	$
International	Surface	$8.00	$8.00	$
	Airmail	$16.00	$16.00	$
	DHL Air	$17.00	$17.00	$

Subtotal _____

CA residents add
applicable sales tax _____

IN, MA and MD
residents add
5% sales tax _____

IL residents add
6.25% sales tax _____

RI residents add
7% sales tax _____

TX residents add
8.25% sales tax _____

Shipping _____

Total _____

Ship to:

Name_____

Address_____

Company_____

City/State/Zip_____

Daytime Phone_____

Payment: ☐ Check to IDG Books (US Funds Only)

☐ Visa ☐ Mastercard ☐ American Express

Card # _____ Exp. _____ Signature_____